WOMEN IN SPORTS

WOMEN
IN SPORTS

Irwin Stambler

DOUBLEDAY & COMPANY, INC.
GARDEN CITY, NEW YORK
1975

Library of Congress Cataloging in Publication Data
Stambler, Irwin.
    Women in sports.

    CONTENTS: Women in sports: the long, hard climb.—
Babe Didrikson Zaharias, superstar: track, field and
golf.—Cathy Rigby: gymnastics. [etc.]
    1. Athletes, Women—United States—Biography—
Juvenile literature. [1. Athletes, Women] I. Title.
GV967.A1S69   796′.019′40922 [B] [920]
ISBN 0-385-07931-1 Trade
    0-385-07426-3 Prebound
Library of Congress Catalog Card Number 74-12713

To Casey Nicole Sprague
and Tomorrow's Women Athletes

Contents

ACKNOWLEDGMENTS

I have been fortunate in working on this book to receive unstinting co-operation from many people and organizations. I would particularly like to thank the following for their invaluable assistance: Wyomia Tyus Simburg; Cathy Rigby; Sally Geis, Braven Dyer and the Citizen Savings Athletic Foundation (formerly Helms Athletic Foundation); NBC Entertainment; International Track Association; Joan Osako and the United States Air Force; Doug Diltz and Carl Byoir & Associates; Philip Morris Inc.; United States Lawn Tennis Association; Immaculata College; Northbrook Skating Club; Santa Anita Race Track; Sunkist Invitational; National Hot Rod Association.

IRWIN STAMBLER

Beverly Hills, California

WOMEN IN SPORTS

1

WOMEN IN SPORTS
The Long, Hard Climb

Until the second half of the 1800s the most strenuous game American women played was croquet. Even then, croquet playing generally was restricted to the genteel, affluent section of society. In Europe, women had started to participate in a more demanding activity, tennis. In 1875, a member of a well-to-do family on Long Island, Mary Ewing Outerbridge, encountered lawn tennis while vacationing in Bermuda. She enjoyed it so much, she bought some rackets and tennis balls and introduced lawn tennis to her friends at home. The game spread like wildfire among young women of wealthy families, and it didn't take long before there were competitive events with dozens of players taking part. By the turn of the century hard fought matches were taking place at national championship meets. (One of the first great U.S. champions, Hazel Hotchkiss Wightman, who won her first tournament in 1902, was still agile and teaching tennis to youngsters in the 1970s.)

But women had begun to make inroads into a number of other sports in the 1900s. Sometimes it was halting progress. For example, as early as 1906 Lula Olive Gill made the record books in California horse racing when she became the first woman jockey to win a race in the state. However, horse racing, which had a history as a competitive sport going back several hundred years, had never encouraged women participants. And even when it became one of the most popular spectator sports in the 1900s, there was little desire to change that. Despite the success of a sprinkling of women riders like Lula Gill, official rules across the United States had no provision for certifying women jockeys. When Robyn Smith challenged this in the 1960s, it took a hard fight lasting a number of years before she could demonstrate her professional caliber on major race tracks.

As the twentieth century moved along women began to adopt costumes for sporting activities more in keeping with the needs of bodily freedom. Within a few decades after the turn of the century, excellent competition in swimming was underway. After World War I, new events were included for women in the re-activated Olympics, and soon stars appeared in such sports as skating, skiing, and track and field. Women's golf joined tennis as a popular activity across the United States.

What equal opportunity might mean to the sports world was underlined in the early 1930s when one of the all-time great athletes burst on the national scene at the 1932 Olympic Games. By any measure, Babe Didrikson ranks as the greatest all-around athlete in sports history. Unlike most women with sports potential, she had the kind of job support often given to men but rarely accorded to women. Because she was hired as a secretary by an athletically minded company with an interest in amateur women's basketball, she had the chance to train properly—the flexibility of her work schedule permitted her to enter the meets that propelled her to stardom.

This kind of backing was rare even in the relatively enlightened post-World War II decades. Though women had made great strides in gaining their rightful place in the sports picture, attitudes in general still hadn't changed much by this period. In a conference dealing with discrimination against women in sports in Los Angeles in 1974, Jean Stapleton of the National Organization for Women pointed to the obstacles still placed in the path of women athletes. "In our society, the qualities of aggressiveness, speed and agility are considered to be male characteristics. Women are discouraged socially and financially from participating in sports."

A fourteen-year-old panelist, Lynn Bright, noted that little girls are supposed to be interested in dolls rather than track or football. By junior high school "you are supposed to be a young lady. Volleyball is acceptable, but girls who wanted to play other sports would be a laughingstock. The guys would look at you and say 'yuk!' especially if you happen to be bigger than they are. Big muscles sure don't get you any dates. Most girls I know think it takes a tomboy to play sports. Our place is supposed to be on the sidelines with pretty smiles."

Seconding Lynn's protests was seventeen-year-old Joyce Wilson, the first girl in Palisades High School

(Pacific Palisades, California) to register for a boys' class in gymnastics. Lack of facilities and coaching, she noted, "starts in the third grade when the boys' and girls' physical education classes split up. That's when the boys take basketball and the girls take jump rope."

One reason most girls accepted a passive role where sports were concerned, one-time sports writer Tom Elias told the meeting, wasn't an inherent dislike of athletics by girls, but rather the lack of positive attitudes by much of the news media toward women athletes. "The basic rules of sports writers is that the best-looking women are singled out for coverage, no matter how badly they play the game." Analyzing an article in a national magazine about a women's tournament, he pointed out the main stress was on the shapely form of the woman who placed sixteenth. "I wonder what kind of descriptive prose, if any, would have been accorded the man who placed sixteenth." He also stressed lack of coverage of women's sports, noting one network that devoted only one hour of 366 hours of live sport coverage to women's activities.

"The result of this paucity of coverage is that women don't get the satisfaction of seeing their accomplishments publicized." Even reasonably good publicity of women in sports, he suggested, could greatly increase the number of girls entering these pursuits by giving them examples to take after.

Elias, Jean Stapleton and other observers agreed that above all it was the financial aspect that contributed to the slow progress of women's sports. In community after community, boards of education, both local and statewide, failed to provide more than token budgets for girls' athletics. Studies of school budgets showed the ratio of boys' to girls' funding in California, for instance, was something like 10–1 in favor of boys' programs. The school board in Syracuse, New York, in 1970 voted $87,000 for boys' programs and nothing for girls'. The same situation applied to colleges. The University of Washington, for instance, had over 40 per cent female enrollment, but less than 1 per cent of the athletic budget was for women's sports.

Many officials rationalized that equal or close to equal funds for both sexes might cause drastic curtailment of boys' sports or seriously impair their confidence in their own abilities! But one even-handed program that was implemented in the state of Iowa provided strong evidence to the contrary—it raised the quality all around. The program was established in 1954 at the Iowa Girls' High School Athletic Union headed by Wayne Cooley, the former assistant to the president of Grinnell College. Cooley worked successfully to establish an equal program—including a promotion program—that made everyone in the state aware of the quality and excitement of women's sports.

By 1974 the fruits of Cooley's crusading efforts were obvious. Close to five hundred high schools had full girls' programs, and thousands of girls took part in league competitions and end-of-season championships in such sports as track, golf, softball, tennis, volleyball, swimming, gymnastics, coed tennis and many others. Attendance for girls' sports compared well with that for boys', and in many cases, doubleheaders were held with a boys' game followed by a girls' or vice versa. In contrast to other states' programs, equipment and facilities for both sexes were equal and coaches for girls' teams received the same pay as did boys' coaches—something not true elsewhere. The result was excellent quality among both groups and an added dimension to athletics in the state that made life more interesting for athletes, parents and friends alike. As fan interest was whetted by newspaper, radio and TV coverage of the women's athletics, gate receipts for girls' games went up radically.

In the late 1960s and early 1970s, medical experts began to look more closely at some of the reasons given for downgrading women's athletics. What about the long-standing claim that sports could be a health hazard? Dr. Clayton L. Thomas of Harvard University, a consultant on human reproduction and a member of the U. S. Olympic Medical and Training Services Committee told *Sports Illustrated*, "The literature of the past contains many opinions stating that competitive events are harmful to women. There are no data, however, to support these negative views."

Prominent medical experts noted that studies indicated that, if anything, the male anatomy was more exposed to injury than the female's. What dangers there were for women, they suggested, could easily be minimized if the athletic goods industry developed protective equipment equal in degree to that available for men. Others conducted analyses that indicated that, just as for boys and men, athletic activity for the most part was a good thing, making a girl or woman stronger and healthier.

The Iowa program, as well as a number of others in which girls had new-found opportunity to take part in sports disproved many of the old bugaboos raised by opponents of increased funding of women's athletics. Given the chance to take part in sports, great numbers of girls turned out to vie for team positions. The competitions resulting from this were as close and spine tingling, as boys' activities, and spectators coming to these events often became strong followers of girls' sports. On a college level, the national basketball tournament sponsored by the newly formed (at the start of the '70s) Association for Intercollegiate Athletics for Women regularly attracted turn-away crowds who marveled at the skill of such women superstars of the sport as Immaculata College's Theresa Shank.

The Olympic Games also indicated the widespread interest in women's athletics, as well as showcasing the wide range of talents women brought to sports. The Games showed the excellent style and form women could achieve in just about any type of athletics in which they received adequate training. The record-shattering efforts of women from Russia and Eastern Europe in the post-World War II Olympics demonstrated what happened when support for women performers approached that for men. The fact that Russia won dual track meets with the United States because of the dominance of their women's team finally caused an increase in backing for U.S. women runners, high jumpers and the like.

Despite all the roadblocks, however, by the mid-1970s it was obvious that women's sports was an idea whose time had come. The shortcomings were many, but the question was not whether full sports equality would come, but just how long it would take to be an accomplished fact. As Patricia Harvey, athletics consultant to Los Angeles city schools told the 1974 National Organization for Women meeting, ". . . in the last five or six years there have been tremendous changes in the attitudes of administrators, parents and the girls themselves towards participation in sports."

As a look at the careers of some of the women in sports, from Babe Didrikson on, clearly shows, a tradition of female excellence in athletics was well-established as the closing decades of the twentieth century moved along.

2

BABE DIDRIKSON ZAHARIAS, SUPERSTAR
Track, Field and Golf

"Woman Athlete of the Half Century!" That's what an Associated Press poll named Babe Didrikson in 1950. A quarter of a century later, there was nothing in evidence to show why she should not eventually be listed as the woman athlete of the century. In fact, from her exploits in a tragically short lifetime, she might well rank as the greatest athlete—male or female —of all time. The tremendous range of sports she mastered has not been equaled by anyone to date, and her performances in track, basketball, baseball, etc., indicate that she could have vied with the male athletes assembled for the TV Superstars' competition. Although it had no bearing on her athletic abilities, she was known as a very fine human being.

Her family traced its roots back to Norway. Her father had served as a ship's carpenter, and after leaving the sea he settled in Port Arthur, Texas, where Babe was born in 1914. (There is some confusion as to whether Babe was a nickname or a given name. Some sports writers state the latter, but the evidence seems to be her real full name was Mildred Ella Didrikson.) When she was three and a half, the family moved to Beaumont and, a little later, to Dallas. Babe spent most of her youthful years in Dallas where she began to show her athletic prowess in high school. She was outstanding as a basketball player and her talents quickly became so well known that Employers Casualty Company of Dallas gave her a job as a secretary in 1930 so the sixteen-year-old could play on their Amateur Athletic Union basketball team.

And did she play! The 5-foot, 6½-inch teen-ager could dribble with either hand and she could out jump girls many inches taller. With Babe as a sparkplug, the Employers Casualty team was a strong contender for national AAU basketball honors and Babe was twice named as a forward to the first All-American team.

The head of Employers Casualty, Colonel M. J. McCombs, was a one-time runner and track enthusiast. He could see immediately that Babe packed tremendous speed and spring in her 126-pound body. He suggested she train for track and field and spent many hours showing her the fine points of a variety of events from the sprints to the high jump and the javelin throw. In 1931, he felt she was ready for major competition and the company sent her to the National AAU Track and Field Championships.

By the end of the first day of women's events, her name was on everybody's lips. She was unbeatable in almost everything she tried. She was, literally, a one-girl track team. She entered nine events and took first place in eight of them, sweeping to victory in the 100-

and 220-yard dashes and the 80-meter hurdles and outstripping the field in the javelin and discus throws, the broad jump and the high jump. In the 50-yard dash she only tied for first! In the shotput she was edged out, finishing second. It was an unbelievable exhibition, but few people beyond those at the meet were aware of it, for women's sports were barely noted in the nation's sports pages.

The next summer, with the 1932 Olympics in view, she returned to action in the National AAU Championships which also served as the Olympic trials. Once more she electrified the audience, this time in Northwestern University's Dycke Stadium, near Evanston, Illinois, with superlative efforts. She entered eight of the ten scheduled events and, as the sole representative of Employers Casualty, scored a total of thirty points. This was enough for her to win the meet title, beating out teams with twenty, thirty or more women per competing team. In a way, it was a letdown. Babe "only" won five events: the 80-meter hurdles, broad jump, javelin, baseball throw (an event long banished from Olympic lists, but a victory that underlined her great skill in this sport), shotput and broad jump. In the course of sweeping those events, the compact Texan, who dared her opponents with the words, "Ahm gonna whup you," set three world records. She also just missed a tie in a sixth event, the high jump.

Olympic rules restricted the number of events one person could compete in to three. Babe chose the 80-meter hurdles, javelin throw and high jump. This choice actually brought her into 60 per cent of the women's track and field events at that Olympics because there were only five of them open to women. This did not include swimming and diving, where such glamorous girls as Georgia Coleman, Jean McSheehey and Eleanor Holm took part, the latter, of course, going on to movie stardom. The arrangement symbolized the attitudes of international sportsmen to women. The Olympics still was conceived as basically a male institution and more attention was paid to the female "form" than to an individual woman's athletic skill. Despite all her great ability, when she arrived in Los Angeles, site of the '32 Summer Games, Babe received scant press attention compared to the members of the swim team.

Once the scene shifted to the huge new Coliseum, built specially for the Olympic Games with a seating capacity of 100,000, Babe came into her own. For the eighteen-year-old, widespread publicity hardly occurred to her as she excitedly entered the huge stadium on opening day in the massed ranks of performers from all corners of the globe. There was a gleam in her gray-green eyes and joy at just being there, as the last of a series of runners brought in the torch that had originally been lighted in Greece and the flame above the peristyle end of the huge oval was lit for the weeks of competition.

Soon after, she tasted the first draughts of victory as she easily went through the preliminary heats of the 80-meter hurdles and sped to victory in the finals for her first gold medal. Fittingly, she set a new world's record in doing this. In the javelin, too, she was unbeatable, sending the slender, arrow-tipped shaft high and far, well beyond the distance it had been thrown by any previous woman athlete. Symbolically, she had proven a champion in an event that had been one of the central ones in the original Olympics over 2,000 years before.

It only remained for her to win the high jump to cap a Cinderella-like appearance. The determined Texan had come from obscurity to capture the hearts of the massed rows of shirt-sleeved fans who jammed the arena every day. Decades later, sports writers who had been small boys then recalled warmly the awe-inspiring feats of the Babe. Nor did she really disappoint them in the high jump. She easily cleared the bar at lower heights and, as one jumper after another dropped out, found herself locked in a duel with Jean Shiley, a girl with considerably more experience in the event than Babe. The bar went to 5 feet, 3 inches and both cleared it. Then it was moved to 5 feet, 5 inches, a height never made by a woman in a sanctioned meet. To rumbles of approval from the crowd, both took turns in soaring over the trembling wand suspended on supports at each end.

The officials then carefully raised the bar to 5 feet, 5¾ inches, and the two girls readied for three more tries to break the deadlock. Both tried mightily to no avail. Jean Shiley came close on her last jump, just grazing the bar as she went over. It vibrated, then fell into the pit. Babe's turn came and she limbered up, then took the short run up, placed her weight on one foot and jumped. She soared high in the air, kicked her lead foot over the bar and followed through in a rolling motion. For a moment, the crowd came to life as it seemed she had made it, then groaned as an almost imperceptible brush caused it to follow her down into the sawdust.

Babe's style was one the officials weren't accustomed to, though it became for many years the dominant one used by almost all high jumpers. Some onlookers from other teams wondered if it was legal. The rules at the time prohibited a diving-type jump, requiring that the jumper's feet always clear the bar before his or her head went over. Up to that point in the competition, though, no one had said anything about Babe's method.

The bar was lowered to 5 feet, 5¼ inches, and both girls asked to have a tie-breaking jump off. This time Jean and Babe both went over on the first try. To Babe's amazement, the judges awarded the match to Jean. Their reason—Babe had jumped illegally, it being claimed, apparently from complaints of others, that Babe's technique constituted a "dive." At any event, it was claimed Babe's head had gone over the bar first, something she and her coach denied vigorously. She still was awarded the silver medal, but most experts felt she should truly have scored three golds in three tries.

Babe's performance won her many friends among sports writers, and from then on her great natural talent was no longer kept secret from the public. She became close friends with one of the greatest, Grantland Rice, who, after the Games, invited her to join a golf foursome that included writer Paul Gallico and Los Angeles Country Club professional, Olin Dutra. This match is credited with kindling a love for golf that eventually made Babe decide to concentrate on the sport.

Meanwhile, Babe demonstrated her prowess in one sport after another. She played tennis with a style that experts agreed compared with the greatest players in the world. She had a strong, powerful swimming stroke and mastered some of the most difficult springboard and platform dives, including a 2½ gainer that would have done honor to Micki King. She sparred with leading fighters and quickly picked up the fine points of footwork, jabbing and punching. She met some of the best-known billiards players and became proficient enough to best them in three-cushion play. At one point she demonstrated to unbelieving onlookers that she could punt and pass a football farther than many top male players.

And that wasn't all. As the 1930s went by she tried her hand at sport after sport and always took to a new game as though she had specialized in it for years. She proved to be an excellent horsewoman, not only showing riding skill but successfully taking part in hard-driving polo matches. On bowling lanes, she often achieved 200 games and over. She was an excellent marksman with a gun, could throw a baseball on a beeline to home plate from deepest center field, could handle a soccer ball with the finesse of a Pelé. By any standard, she was *the* superathlete.

Through all of this, Babe fought to maintain her amateur status. Though she took part in many sports activities and became a nationally known figure, she received no pay for her athletic efforts. Though she always played to win, she thought of sports as something she did because she enjoyed it, rather than as a way of earning a living.

So it was that the thought of turning professional had not occurred to her when she made her first sally into the golfing world by entering the Ft. Worth, Texas, Women's Invitational in early 1935. She hoped it would be the first step toward becoming state champion. From the moment she stepped out on the first tee and drove the ball over 200 yards down the fairway, excitement rose among the audience. Her first day's score was a fine one and led to the headlines in Texas papers, one of which read, "Wonder Girl Makes Her Debut in Tournament Golf; Turns in 77 Score."

However, her joy soon turned to gloom when the AAU declared her a professional later in the year. Ironically, the edict resulted from an incident not of her making—her picture was used in an advertisement without her permission. However, if she stayed out of competition for three years, she was told, she could regain her amateur status. Dutifully she complied, deciding that when she returned to sports she would make golf her main activity.

During the years of waiting, she doggedly worked to develop a golf game second to none. Every morning on weekdays, barring rain or storm, she was out on the golf course for hours before reporting for work at Employers Casualty. She could be seen slamming incredibly long drives from tee after tee, carefully studying the course layouts to sharpen her technique with the series of clubs known as woods and irons, spending long periods of time on practice greens working on her putting skills. After work she would go out again, walking countless miles over Dallas golf courses until she could have played them almost blindfolded. It was usually the same on weekends and many holidays as well.

Finally, the suspension was lifted in 1938 and Babe was soon on the way toward the golf hall of fame. The year 1938 was a good one for her in more ways than one, and golf played a part in it. During a Los Angeles tournament, she joined a threesome that included a massive, well-muscled man named George Zaharias, considered one of the best in the wrestling field. The two were attracted to one another and married soon after. It was a storybook union; they complemented each other well and remained devoted to each other throughout their married life.

Years later, George recalled, "My fondest memory was every minute I was with her. Just for her to touch me. She had big, beautiful hands and long fingers. She had a touch that would electrify you . . . And we communicated."

From then on, George was rarely away when Babe was competing. As the years went by, he shared many moments of triumph as Babe dominated the women's golf field as no one had before or after. From the moment she stepped back on the tournament trail in 1938 until she finished her playing days abruptly many years later, she was always a challenger. She won eighty-two tournaments in her career and might have won more if World War II hadn't cut down on athletic activities during the first half of the 1940s.

The year the war finally came to a close and people could once more devote close attention to the sports pages, Babe's name often met the eye as she won one golf meet after another on the way to becoming American champion. She was selected as Female Athlete of the Year by the Associated Press, the second time she was so honored. (The first was for her 1932 Olympic achievements.) Her achievements over the next two years were even more sensational. In tournament golf she was all but invincible, winning seventeen straight in 1946–47, a mark no one has come close to since. In 1947, she announced she would go to Gullane, Scotland, to try to become the first American woman ever to win the British Women's Amateur crown.

Over 5,000 people, one of the largest crowds in that event's history, jammed the rolling greens to see if England and Scotland's best could withstand this overseas challenge. As the days went by, it became apparent it would take superlative golf to beat the dynamic Texan. The final day of the tournament found Babe matched with Scotland's top woman golfer, Jean Donald. It turned out to be a mismatch; Babe set a course record in claiming the trophy. At year end, the Associated Press poll again resulted in Babe's being named female athlete of '47, as she had been for 1946. Even the Babe couldn't keep up such a torrid pace and though she won more than she lost the next few years, she didn't win them all. Still, she remained the number one woman golfer into the early '50s, doing well enough in 1950 to gain her fifth Female Athlete of the Year award from the AP.

She was still the one to beat in women's golf in 1953 when she found herself suffering strange pains in her back. She entered a Beaumont, Texas, hospital for observation and the sports world was dismayed to hear that she had to undergo a lengthy operation for cancer. It was fervently hoped she would recover, but few thought she would be able to return to the pressure and the demanding grind of the golf circuit. For several months she lay in a hospital bed with George constantly by her side. Then she was discharged and in short order was out practicing again. In mid-summer, she went to hot, humid Chicago to enter the All-America Open at the famed Tam O'Shanter course. She was a little off her game, but she still did amazingly well. She didn't win, but placed a strong third. She rapidly regained her touch, though, and before the year was over had taken first place in the Sarasota, Florida, Open and the Beaumont, Texas, Babe Didrikson Open. The sports world paid tribute to her gallantry by awarding her the Ben Hogan Trophy for Greatest Comeback of the Year.

She did even better in 1954, winning tournament after tournament including the National Women's Open, the All-America at Tam O'Shanter and the Vare Trophy. For the sixth time the AP poll named her the year's top woman athlete. And she started off 1955 equally well, vanquishing strong opposition from women many years her junior to take the Tampa, Florida, Open and the Serbin Women's Invitational in Miami, Florida.

But she was beginning to feel ominous pain in her back again. Sometimes the pain grew so intense it was hard to rivet her gaze on the ball for an approach shot or a putt. Finally it could no longer be ignored. She went back to the hospital and underwent new examinations. The verdict was not promising. The doctors found new evidence of cancer. Another operation was performed and for a while it seemed she might beat the odds once more.

It was not to be, though she never gave up hope until the last. The cancer relentlessly spread despite the best the doctors could do. George Zaharias stayed close to her over the months, often staying in her room around the clock. They talked about plans for the future, about doings in the world, about sports. One result was a perpetual trophy in her name.

As Zaharias told a Los Angeles *Times* reporter in 1972, "Babe was in the hospital, two months from dying and she brought up the fact that she had won the [female athlete] title six times but never had anything to show for it except press clippings. I got to thinking about it and asked her if she'd like to give a trophy. 'Honey, I'd love it,' she replied.'" The four-foot-high Babe Didrikson Zaharias Trophy has since been awarded by AP to such international stars as Australia's Evonne Goolagong (tennis) and Russia's Olga Korbut (gymnastics).

Babe's condition got worse and she slipped into a coma. George went down for some coffee at 6 A.M. one day, but then "something went through me and I left the coffee and all and went up to the room. She woke up just long enough to say good-by by lifting one finger.

"They want to make a movie of our life. But all they want to do is Babe's records. The story is Babe and me. But *Love Story* already has been done and that's our story."

3

CATHY RIGBY
Gymnastics

For several hundred years, gymnastics ranked as a major sport in Europe. First men and then women throughout that continent adopted it in great numbers as a combination of exercise and competition. Later, as the nations of the Far East entered the international sphere of athletics, they too quickly developed countless teams and many outstanding performers. The sport developed more slowly in the United States, but by the time the modern Olympics began in 1896 American men could provide a reasonably good showing and this pattern has remained into the twentieth century.

On the other hand, U.S. women lagged behind, and rarely were American women's teams in contention in major meets. But the growing awareness of women's rights and need for independence began to change this after World War II. In 1956, Muriel Grossfeld provided the nation with its first world-caliber female gymnast with a good performance in the Olympic Games. Her efforts at the 1960 and '64 Games also were fine ones, though not good enough for the very top levels. But it indicated a quickening of interest that was reflected in the start of a number of women's gymnastics clubs and the appearance by the mid-1960s on the world scene of such excellent performers as Linda Metheny, Roxanne Pierce and Kim Chace. As the decade came to a close, the slight form of Cathy Rigby emerged from obscurity to carry American women's gymnastics to new heights.

Little Cathy's exploits excited the imagination of girls throughout the nation, starting a groundswell of gymnastic activity that promises to make the United States a major contender for international honors before the 1970s are over. In 1973, for instance, sales of such equipment as balance beams, side horses, uneven parallel bars and tumbling mats for women's gymnastics went up by 50 per cent in the United States. By 1973 the number of girls taking part in high school sponsored programs doubled to 35,000 from an estimated 17,000 in 1970, and where there had been only ten or fifteen clubs in existence in 1970, by 1973 there were over six hundred, with girls and women from eight to eighteen participating.

As Muriel Grossfeld pointed out, it was not so much the lack of interest in past years that kept down women's gymnastics as it was the lack of facilities and capable teachers. "When I was competing," she said, "none of the best girls had coaches. We all trained ourselves. Now at least our good ones are getting proper training. But there still are not enough well-trained coaches. You can count the good ones on your hand."

Cathy Rigby was lucky in that sense. When she decided to try gymnastics in 1963 at the age of ten, there was one of the few top-flight clubs in the nation right near her home. The Southern California Acrobatic Team, or SCATS, had just been started in Long Beach by Bud Marquette, a one-time U.S. gymnastics champion in the 1930s. It was a labor of love. Financial rewards were few, and Marquette and his assistants all earned their livings at other jobs. As he told a reporter, "I started a girl's gymnastics club because they're always being put down. Boys have so much going for them in sports—football, basketball, baseball."

Cathy, the daughter of an aeronautical engineer, Paul Rigby, then working at Douglas Aircraft Company, was born in Long Beach on December 12, 1952. Small from birth, for several years she fought a succession of ills that threatened her life. She was born with collapsed lungs and later was almost laid low by a series of bouts with pneumonia and bronchitis. Her constitution proved stronger than it seemed, though, and after her fifth year she remained healthy and became increasingly active. She learned to ride a bicycle, roller skated and did other things that required a lot of energy. At times, she seemed to her friends to be almost always in motion, running, jumping, moving about constantly.

In the early '60s, her father took her to a trampoline class and she took to it with abandon. The first time she got onto the springy canvas surface she tested it out with a few jumps, then went into increasingly more daring moves under the eye of a tumbling coach. Before the night was over, she had performed several backflips. In succeeding classes, she demonstrated more and more acrobatic ability, so much so that the teacher told Mr. Rigby he should enroll her in Marquette's SCATS.

Marquette has only vague memories of his first meeting with her. But it took only a short time for Cathy to gain the attention of the entire SCATS staff. "At first, of course, we only knew her name. It didn't take long, however, before we realized we had something special. She adapted so easily. She learned so readily. First she only could do a few cartwheels, but in a few weeks she was doing things that girls we'd been working with for years had trouble with."

Not only did Cathy demonstrate inherent talent for acrobatics, she also showed her coaches she had the determination needed for any champion. She was willing to give up almost all other activities to concentrate hour after hour, week after week on strengthening her muscles and developing technique. She went over each routine countless times, smoothing over the rough spots and making even the most complex series of somersaults, flips, handstands and the like practically automatic.

Every day after school she would come to the SCATS gym and work out under the watchful eye of Marquette and his assistants. Each week she added new things to her repertoire. She started by learning the compulsory exercises, things like a forward jump to a handstand; a neck "kip" (beginning with the weight on the back of the neck) to a stand, squat or a half turn to a momentary handstand; multiple somersaults; splits; half-on half-off vaults on the side horse and dozens of others. After she had mastered the basics, she went on to develop intricate routines for the free exercise part of the program. First she studied and developed advanced exercises used by others in the sport and, in time, she added special nuances of her own.

To make it in the sport required seven days a week of effort. When she was not at the gym, she often was practicing at home. The family, too, became involved. Her father and her mother set their own schedule around Cathy's needs. They sold the family piano to get money to buy a set of uneven parallel bars. Practice areas were set aside inside the house and in the yard. For Cathy's beam work, her father built the narrow, elevated four-inch platform on which she was soon performing dazzling splits, handstands, flips and one-foot stands.

To some of her classmates, her single-minded dedication might have seemed curious. When she started gymnastics, of course, she was only ten, and social activities weren't too much on anyone's mind. But as the years went by and she entered her early teens, her friends were attending school affairs, gathering for slumber parties and developing friendships with members of both sexes. For Cathy, it was a steady run of sweat, hours spent in her own separate world, a world made up of journeys up and down that narrow four-inch-wide beam; across a square of springy floor mat; up, down and around a set of shiny bars.

At the time, the chance of eventual financial success was remote; gymnastics was about as amateur a sport as there was. And personal prestige also seemed unlikely, for only a few sports commentators or reporters paid much attention to gymnastics during those years. But, as Jim Fontaine, head of another major Southern

California gymnastics clubs, the KIPS (Keep in Perfect Shape) points out, "Gymnastics has more to offer than other individual sports like swimming and track and field. It's tough training, but it's fun. In gymnastics, there's always something new, always a challenge. A swimmer can only swim faster and a high jumper jump higher. But a gymnast has fun. The girls love to swing on the bars. The challenge of adding another twist or flip to their programs is always there. And if a girl is successful in competition, she has the chance to travel and make the national and Olympic team."

Cathy never regretted the tremendous effort needed to bring her gymnastic success. "It was always a privilege to be in gymnastics," she told the author in 1974. "I never felt I was giving up anything. So many kids just long for a chance to get involved in something like this. I never had to fight to achieve it; it was just there."

In her case, her intense desire paid off soon enough. "I was competing after about seven months," she says. "though my first time out was less than satisfying. At the time, my girl friend and I were the only ones on our team who didn't get a ribbon." Before long, though, Cathy was one of the more successful younger members of SCATS, winning trophies and medals for her age group in many local and state meets. She expanded her scope in 1967. "I performed in my first major meet that year, the Midwest Open in Chicago. I just decided to enter it and my dad took me there. I placed second overall in my age group."

From then on, she traveled to prestige meets in many places with SCATS, exhibiting steadily better performances and a coolness under pressure vital to success in major competition. As the trials for selecting the American team for the 1968 Olympics in Mexico City neared, more and more experts looked at young Cathy as a prime candidate.

Cathy, only 15 and looking even younger with her slim build and small size of barely 4 feet, 10 inches, faced opponents with four to five years more experience. However, her performance at the trials in the spring of '68 was a mature one. She won many marks of 9 or better, in some cases wrenching almost perfect scores of 9.8 or 9.9 from the tough-minded judges. As Russia's Olga Korbut did four years later, Cathy captivated the crowd, winning rippling waves of applause for some of her difficult maneuvers and a standing ovation when each routine was ended.

With Cathy and Linda Metheny as team members, most observers agreed the United States had its best women's gymnastic squad in history. The TV coverage of the trials and Cathy's part in them began to attract national attention to the sport and to bring new fame to those taking part in it. Viewers throughout the United States anxiously watched the proceedings from Mexico City as Cathy, Linda and their cohorts went up against the best the world had to offer. Because other nations provide financial aid in one form or another to permit women to continue in gymnastics as long as they retain top skills, the opposition included many girls with far greater experience than anyone on the American team.

"I was real excited to go," says Cathy. "Probably

the most thrilling time of my whole career in gymnastics was making the team."

The U.S. group gained no medals. Indeed, no women's gymnastic team from this country had ever gained a medal in international championships at that time. But their performances were first rate, earning admiration from knowledgeable fans and generally good scores from the judges. When competition was over, Linda Metheny while not winning a medal, had made it into the finals in the balance beam.

"I was satisfied with my performance," Cathy notes. "I placed seventh in the balance beam and sixteenth overall. It was wonderful to appear before such a large and interested crowd. I didn't worry so much about all those people in the stands as about pleasing the judges. There's a part of the judging called 'general impression' which has an allowance of 1.5 points. That's a pretty vital amount when you consider the spread between first and sixth place could be ³⁄₁₀ of a point."

All in all, Cathy's sixteenth finish was an outstanding accomplishment against the acknowledged superstars of the Russian, Czechoslovakian, Hungarian and German teams.

Cathy paused but slightly to take in a little of the Olympic atmosphere. In a few days time she was back home in California, once more devoting eight hours or more every day of the week to her training. The relative success at Mexico City was only the first stepping stone to what Marquette and his staff confidently expected to be a brilliant series of achievements.

Their confidence was well placed. During 1969, Cathy placed high in many meets both at home and abroad, winning her share and showing growing skill in all four events. More important, she added moves to her floor exercises, side horse vaulting and uneven bars that brought her scores in those classes more in line with that of her best event, the balance beam. The prime goal was the 1972 Olympics, but an important stop on the way was the World Games held in Ljubljana, Yugoslavia in 1970. This was the world series of gymnastics, attended by the same stars who generally made the Olympic teams. A good score in Yugoslavia was almost the equal of an Olympic victory.

Though Cathy had improved in other events, the balance beam was the one that held out the most hope for a medal. But she was up against such great artists as Ludmila Turishcheva and Tamara Lazakovitch of Russia and Karin Janz of East Germany. Cathy gave an almost flawless performance in the preliminaries and easily made the finals. When Cathy arrived in position for her balance beam try, she won a rousing ovation from the crowd. Marks in the high 9s were common and she knew she would have to outdo herself to place in the top five. She saluted the crowd, then mounted the bar and swung into a series of incredibly graceful, intricate maneuvers. She moved across the bar executing handstands, splits, straddles, then balanced on one foot and bent forward with one hand holding her other leg almost straight into the air to make a 90-degree angle with the beam surface. She followed with other smooth flowing motions, climaxed by a soaring dismount. She bowed to the crowd and accepted deafening applause and shouts of approval. Moments later all eyes were on the judges table. The five experts from different countries raised their cards to show a string of high marks—9.8s and 9.9s. The lowest and highest were eliminated and the results soon flashed on the scoreboard. Cathy and her well wishers held their breaths. They knew a few tenths of a point spelled the difference between a fine showing and a disappointment.

But the letters glowed brightly with a 9.9 plus. It seemed good enough for at least the top five bracket. And, soon after, when the last entrants finished their performances, it proved to be so. When all the marks were in, Cathy had beaten both Janz and Turishcheva. She didn't quite take first, but she had taken second and a silver medal, the first ever won by a woman from the United States in world championship competition.

Cathy's eyes were wet with tears as she accepted the medal after the meet was over. Tens of millions of TV viewers around the world understood the emotion as the flag of the United States moved high in the Yugoslavian sports hall with those of two European countries. There were no more medals won by U.S. performers that time, but that one silver was an amazing breakthrough.

As the early '70s proceeded, Cathy continued to give excellent performances all over the world. She was a finalist in almost every meet she took part in, which included major meetings in Tokyo, Japan; Johannesburg, South Africa; London; and several series in Communist nations.

In the spring of 1971, she traveled to Riga, formerly in Latvia but now part of the Soviet Union, for a triangular meet with Russia and Czechoslovakia. In fine form she led the U.S. team with tingling routines in not only the balance beam but in every category. She won high 9s for almost everything she did. When the competition was over, she had placed first on the beam, third on the bars and had a total all-around score good enough for the bronze medal.

Though the experts rated her number one in the United States, she had to fight to hold the honor, particularly against the challenge of Linda Metheny, who beat her in two Amateur Athletic Union meetings, including a slim two tenths of a point margin in the last AAU competition before the '72 Olympics. Cathy asserted herself strongly in the Olympic semifinals in early 1972, beating out Linda to win the meet and move on to the finals in May, a seeming cinch for the trip to Munich later in the year.

Cathy began with a beautiful performance on the side horse to start the compulsory phase on the first day. On the second day she was on her way to extending her lead with a fast-paced workout on the parallel bars when disaster struck. She finished her blinding series of twists and turns with an extended straddle on the high bar, the last move before dismount. But her arms slipped ever so slightly, causing one toe to drop down an inch or two until it caught beneath the bar. She lost her hold and fell straight down as an official rushed to try and protect her head from the floor. She escaped with only a toe fracture, but to many onlookers it seemed the injury plus her scoring loss might cost her the chance to make the team. The judges gave her an average of 8.3, far below the 9.8 she probably would have earned otherwise. She fell to second place.

Cathy showed her great courage and iron will by coming back. She maintained poise and control as things got underway the next day and began chipping away at the lead. She moved past Linda Metheny in the first event when the latter missed a step and fell from the beam. In the next category, floor exercises, Cathy followed with a good series of flips, giant splits, one arm handstands, somersaults and the like. But the crowd groaned when she moved off the mat after taking her bow. She was obviously limping. It had happened on her first exercise, an "Arabian," a half-turned front flip. After completing it, when her foot hit the mat she heard a popping noise in her ankle. Though she felt weakness in the ankle, she managed to finish and did well enough to retain first place at day's end by a tenth of a point. But X rays showed she had damaged ankle ligaments. She had to miss the fourth day and Roxanne Pierce took first.

Her performance to that point had been so good and her presence was so important to U.S. hopes that the Olympic committee elected her to the team anyway. She responded gratefully by going back into training barely a week after the accident. However, the mishap probably took something out of her.

From TV and most sports reports, a casual observer might conclude the U.S. team at Munich did only fairly well. The performances of Cathy and her team members were overshadowed by the overwhelming success of the Russians, who unveiled not only their long-established stars, but another performer, young Olga Korbut.

Cathy agrees Olga deserved the accolades, but she

points out that the U.S. media failed to balance this with proper attention to American accomplishments. "The U.S. team at Munich did the best in our history. We placed fourth as a team, the closest we ever got to a medal. You didn't hear about that in the United States. Our girls did things never done before and got no credit. I can understand in pro sports it might be proper to say 'why didn't you win?' but in amateur sports, and the Olympics in particular, it's important to praise good results even if athletes don't come in first. If you don't, the kids will just feel left out and there won't be the encouragement needed to attract new young people to the sport."

As for Cathy, while she didn't win a medal, she too improved greatly on her 1968 effort. Just before the last event, she was in seventh place overall, even ahead of Olga Korbut. Her final finish was tenth, but that was six places better than in '68, and she placed seventh in the balance beam.

After the '72 Olympics, Cathy retired from amateur competition. She put her acrobatic skills to work in 1974 in the title role of the NBC Entertainment version of the classic *Peter Pan*. Backstage before rehearsals, she gave freely of her time to teach cast members some of the fine points of gymnastics. She also worked for progress in the field through exhibitions and by helping to instruct some of the eager young athletes who wanted to follow in her footsteps.

4

BILLIE JEAN KING
Tennis

The date was September 20, 1973, and the eyes of the United States and, indeed, much of the world literally were focused on the Houston Astrodome. Was it a championship baseball game, a classic football match up, a world heavyweight contest? No, the attraction was a tennis game, perhaps the game of the century from a publicity standpoint. The participants were a fifty-five-year-old man and a graceful twenty-nine-year-old woman. It was a game that had no impact at all on the sports record book, but a great deal of importance for the cause of women in sports. The man, of course, was Bobby Riggs and his opponent the redoubtable Billie Jean King.

As Billie Jean was aware, it was a situation, apart from defending women's honor, where she had more to lose than to win. Riggs, a one-time champion, had been out of the public eye for over a decade when he "hustled" himself back into the spotlight by claiming that even an over-the-hill male tennis expert could defeat the best women players of the period. He bolstered his contention by defeating Australian champion, Margaret Smith Court, then called for the number one woman player of the time, Billie Jean, to accept his challenge. Win or lose against her, he would remain a new-found celebrity as well as gaining a small fortune. Even if he lost, few could dispute that he had done as much as anyone could expect, under the circumstances, from a man in his mid-fifties.

For Billie Jean, it posed the danger that her brilliance as one of the great all-time women players might be dimmed. If she lost, people might forget her many victories in the most prestigious tournaments of the tennis world and remember only that she was beaten by a man twenty-six years her senior.

It was not something to be taken lightly, for Billie Jean had devoted almost her entire life to tennis. Her career had gotten underway at about the time that Riggs's great years were drawing to a close. Born in 1944, Billie Jean Moffitt came from an athletically talented family. (Her brother later pitched for the San Francisco Giants professional baseball team.) Growing up in Long Beach, California, she demonstrated ability with a tennis racket before she reached her teens. By the time she was in high school, she could defeat opponents years older than she was, and word of her potential began to filter around the tennis field.

In her mid-teens, she could already show opponents a blistering, accurate serve and a high backhand shot that was to remain her strong point throughout her career. At sixteen, she was playing in important tennis tournaments in the United States and in 1961, at seventeen, she made her debut at England's fabled

Wimbledon, the most coveted tournament of them all. It was an exciting time for a young, eager player, particularly when she was assigned the glamorous center court for her first round match. However, her opponent, far more experienced, won the day and Billie Jean was only a spectator for the rest of the event.

But a year can make a big difference. Playing in almost every important tournament after the '61 Wimbledon, Billie Jean built up her poise and confidence. Everyone agreed she was a much improved player when she again went to London the following year. Her hopes were given a jolt, though, when she was paired with Margaret Smith for the opening round, again on the desired center court. Ms. Smith, twenty years old in 1962, was rated the number one player in the world that year and a heavy favorite to take the women's singles competition at Wimbledon. But she never got past the first round. The gallery was treated to some of the best tennis they'd seen as the two battled back and forth with first Ms. Smith and then Billie Jean having the advantage. The first two sets were split, then Billie Jean broke through to win the third and deciding match.

It was the start of a rivalry that was to continue unabated into the early 1970s, often ending with these two competing in the final match at such places as Wimbledon or at the U.S. championships at Forest Hills, New York. From 1962 through 1973, Billie Jean never missed the decisive rounds at Wimbledon. Over that time span, she reached the finals eight times, semifinals twice and quarterfinals twice.

In the 1963 finals, Margaret Smith served notice she wouldn't give up her crown to the younger player without a battle, defeating Billie Jean in straight sets. In 1964, the Australian won out over the American every time they met and the following year turned back Billie Jean in the U.S. singles finals at Forest Hills. Ms. King was winning her share of tournaments, but it was still hard to make up the extra years of top-flight play Margaret Smith Court had under her belt.

With each passing year, though, Billie Jean was catching up, polishing her blistering backhand and strong forehand and increasing the stamina that let her roam across the court to return shots at the net one moment, then from the deep corner the next. Such stars as Rosemary Casals and Nancy Richey Gunter challenged her for top U.S. honors, but had to fight hard to even win a set against Billie Jean's increasingly flawless style. In 1966, Ms. King returned to Wimbledon at the peak of her game and easily moved through the early rounds. In the semis, she was again on center court against Margaret Smith. As usual, the fans were shown outstanding tennis as both women demonstrated almost every shot in the book—overhead lobs, forehand and backhand smashes, mid-court drop shots with tricky backspin. With all her great skill, though, Ms. Court was no match for Billie Jean on that day. When it was over, the compact, bespectacled brunette from the West Coast felt she had proven she was the top woman player in the world. Many experts wouldn't concede that, and she wasn't ranked number one during 1967 and '68 even though Margaret Smith Court retired almost the whole two years.

By the end of the 1960s, when Margaret Court returned to action, Billie Jean also found growing competition from many promising newcomers, including teen-agers Chris Evert from the United States and Evonne Goolagong from Australia. But on any given day, when Billie Jean was in top form in the demanding, tricky sport, she was usually unbeatable. The fact that she tended to be downgraded by some authorities was thought by some to be a reflection on her sometimes controversial stands rather than her ability. She was outspokenly in favor of bettering the lot of women in all ways. She was also against what she considered the hypocrisy of so-called amateur athletics and played a key role in expanding the open concept of tournament play where tennis experts could be professionals and still compete for the great honor of winning Wimbledon or Forest Hills.

She took pains to note that she was not anti-male; she was, after all, Mrs. King. Rather she wanted women to have the chance for equal opportunity in sports. As she told reporters, she began playing tennis because it was a sport where she could make maximum use of her talent and still be considered feminine. By succeeding in tennis under those conditions she also felt she was helping to disprove the old ideas that a girl athlete had to seem more like a man than a woman.

In the matter of professionalism, she was equally bold in expressing her views. As she told *Sports Illustrated,* "No matter how small it is, if they are given financial aid for excelling at sport, calling them amateurs is incorrect. As an amateur tennis player, whether they gave me $10 or $4,000 under the table, I still considered myself a professional and I didn't like being called an amateur. The amateur ideal is ridiculous; I think finally we have realized that amateurism in the Olympics is a farce. Well, tennis was like that for a thousand years. The word always has been that amateurs play sport for the love of it. Listen, professionals love it just as much, probably more so. We put our lives on the line for sport."

The end of the 1960s, Billie Jean played a key role in beginning the most important development in professional tennis for women, the Virginia Slims tournament. She was the first major star to sign up for it and actively encouraged other players to join. With the Virginia Slims firm supplying hundreds of thousands of dollars in prize money for an annual series of tournaments all over the United States, women tennis stars finally had the chance to earn rewards at least partly in line with what had been available to male players for a number of years before.

At first, Margaret Court did not join the Virginia Slims tour. After possibly her best year ever in 1970—she won all the tournaments in the tennis "Grand Slam" including a cliff-hanging two-and-a-half-hour win over Billie Jean at Wimbledon—she retired again in 1971 to have a baby. This took a little of the luster from Billie Jean's outstanding year on the tour. During '71, she won $117,000, the first woman tennis player ever to have winnings over $100,000. Billy Jean won many other important victories in 1971, but nineteen-year-old Evonne Goolagong took the Wimbledon crown and, despite Billie Jean's greatest year ever, she was ranked second for the year.

With that incentive, Billie Jean decided that 1972 had to be her year. During the winter, she scored impressive tournament wins over Nancy Gunter, Kerry Melville of Australia and her 1971 Wimbledon nemesis, Evonne Goolagong. Her game seemed to become even stronger and more sparkling as the months went by. By the time the dates for Wimbledon neared, Billie Jean had captured the American and French singles championships, two of the three titles needed for a "Big Three" sweep. A Wimbledon victory would place her name in the record books with only a handful of other great players.

For all that, when she arrived in England for Wimbledon, she was seeded second behind Goolagong, and some experts thought Chris Evert, seventeen, and still an amateur, might top both of them. Chris, in fact, was the "Cinderella" of the tournament, and even English fans were rooting for her when she collided with Evonne Goolagong in the semifinals. After Chris won the first set, though, the "veteran" Goolagong, twenty years old, fought back to take the next two sets and move into the finals against Billie Jean. Billie Jean had turned back a series of rivals with ease to enter the Wimbledon finals for the seventh time.

When Evonne and Billie Jean took the court for their championship rematch, the stands were packed and expectant. The crowd gave a rousing reception to the lithe young Australian, but was decidedly cool when Billie Jean moved into position. The crowd applauded vigorously as Evonne scored with several well-placed shots against her American challenger. There was a series of "line calls" by the officials that all went against Billie Jean, causing some U.S. reporters to complain of possible bias. (A line call is a decision by the referee on whether a ball landing near the boundary lines of the court is "in" and a fair ball or "out.") This, coupled with the unfriendly crowd added tremendous pressure to an already tense situation. But Billie Jean refused to get rattled. Shrugging off some close scoring losses, she stuck to her game plan, making Evonne move from one side of the court to the other to return well placed shots, then catching her rival out of position to get to a sharply placed cannonball or an overhead lob.

The first set was no contest, as Billie Jean vanquished Evonne six games to three. The partisan crowd hoped Evonne could come back in the second set as she had done against Chris Evert, and for a brief moment as it started, it looked as though she might when she took some of the first games with some beautiful cross-court forehand strokes. But Billie Jean steadied and took the match going away, 6–3, for a two-set sweep.

Of course, Margaret Court had not taken part. But later in the year she returned to action on the Virginia Slims tour and easily turned back Goolagong, Evert and Melville in a number of events. Against Billie Jean, though, it was another story. The two ended up in the finals in four tournaments and each won a pair. In a fifth event at Forest Hills, the two graced opposite sides of the net in the semifinals. Billie Jean swept the match, 6–4, 6–4, and ended up with an edge in the overall series with Margaret for the year.

When 1972 came to a close, no one could doubt that Billie Jean was the queen of the tennis world and one of the top athletes of the year in any sport. She won many awards for her achievements, including being named Sportswoman of the Year by *Sports Illustrated*.

Billie Jean took off the last few months of 1972. During that period, Margaret Smith Court demonstrated anew her great ability by dominating the Virginia Slims program. By early 1973, Margaret had won ten of twelve tournaments on the tour. At the top of her game, Ms. Court accepted a challenge to play Bobby Riggs. For some time, Riggs had mounted a massive publicity campaign whose theme was that women's liberation was aimed at downgrading men and "destroying their egos." He would help defeat this insidious campaign, he shrilled, by winning the male vs. female match of the century. He tried to line up a match with Billie Jean, saying, "If she can't beat a tired old man, she doesn't deserve half her dough." Billie Jean didn't rise to the bait, knowing, as Bobby did, that it was really a put-on designed to give Bobby a strange kind of comeback chance.

However, as she smilingly said after the Court-Riggs match was arranged, "If Margaret loses, we're in trouble. I'll have to challenge him myself."

The match took place on Mother's Day, 1973, on a sun-drenched court in Ramona, California, near the city of San Diego. A close score was expected, though most observers thought Margaret Court would finally win. But a nationwide TV audience was treated to a surprising turn of events. Riggs put on a display of cool, seasoned tennis. He no longer could hit slashing drives to the base line or storm the net, but was able to precisely control placement of the ball and confused Ms. Court with a wide range of "junk" shots—high overhead lobs that just stayed inside the line, short placements with tremendous backspin, slicing shots that kept Margaret constantly moving and off balance for a good return. His approach destroyed her concentration and resulted in an easy win for him, 6–2, 6–1.

Now there was no doubt that Bobby would meet Billie Jean. And the already great interest built up in the Court-Riggs battle promised to develop into the biggest excitement over a single tennis match in the sport's history. It was finally agreed that Billie Jean and Riggs would face each other in the huge Houston Astrodome in Texas which could seat five to ten times as many people as the largest regular tennis arena. There was brisk bidding for TV rights with ABC winning out and assigning the blunt-talking Howard Cosell to anchor the reporting team that would cover the event for an expected 50 million viewers.

Before the September confrontation with the man now called the number one male chauvinist pig was finalized, Billie Jean had some other business to attend to at Wimbledon in July. Demonstrating superlative technique, she turned back Evonne Goolagong in the semifinals to set up a title fight with Chris Evert. Chris, who won over Margaret Court to reach the finals, had badly beaten Billie Jean in Boca Raton, Florida, the previous October, just before Ms. King went off on vacation. This time things were different. With a stunning series of angle shots, Billie Jean swept the first set 6–0 and stood off a determined counter-attack by Chris in the second set to win 7–5. For the fifth time, Billie Jean had won the beautifully engraved silver plate that symbolized Wimbledon women's champion. It represented the greatest number of Wimbledon titles gained by a woman since the pre-World War II years. "Now," said Billie Jean, waving it above her head, "I'm ready for Bobby."

The scene at the Astrodome in September was spectacular. Over 30,000 people, the largest ever to watch a tennis match, ringed the green synthetic court stretched over the second- and third-base lines of the Houston baseball team's diamond. Both Billie Jean and Bobby arrived in the style expected for a $100,000, winner-take-all event. Bobby was brought onto the court drawn over a gold carpet in a ricksha pulled by eight good-looking girls in red shorts. Billie Jean was preceded by a group of strapping men holding aloft plumes on long sticks and was carried in a litter borne on the shoulders of another four athletically built males.

Up to the point that the two took up their stances across the white net, the atmosphere was more of a circus than a sport. However, once Billie Jean launched the first ball diagonally across into the white enclosed serve area on Bobby's side, the strain of the occasion quickly showed on the players' faces. Billie Jean took the first game, but Bobby fought back to win the next one convincingly, and many who had accepted the odds makers' quotes of 5–2 in favor of the male contender smiled knowingly. (A set in tennis is decided by a series of "games," with each player alternately serving for an entire game. A player serves in each game until a minimum of three points has been scored. However, the game is not decided until one player has achieved a two-point margin over the other. The first player to win six games wins the set, but only if the edge is at least two games. Thus, if one player is ahead 5 games to 4 and wins the next game, he or she wins the set 6–4. But if the opponent wins to make it 5–5, then it would take two more straight games for one or the other to win. Under recently introduced professional rules, should the score go to 6–6, however, the winner would be decided by a single tie-breaker game.)

As the match progressed, it was obvious Bobby wouldn't be able to run away from Billie Jean as he had from Ms. Court. Billie Jean won the third game and Bobby the fourth to square things at two games each. There seemed a possible turning point when Bobby broke through Billie Jean's serve in the fifth game to take a 3–2 lead. However, Billie Jean came back to win the next game even though it was Bobby's turn to serve. Gaining confidence as the service returned to her, she hit shot after shot that kept Bobby rushing from one side of the green surface to the other until his clothes were soaked with perspiration. She took her second game in a row with ease to make it 4–3 in her favor. Bobby fought back to tie at four all, but he was obviously tiring. In short order, Billie Jean took the last two games to win the set 6–4.

From then on, it was no contest even though the match was based on the best three sets out of five men's tournament rules rather than the two sets out of three of women's competition. Billie Jean took the next two sets in convincing fashion, 6–3, 6–3.

Afterward, Bobby congratulated Billie Jean. "She was just too quick. I couldn't get the ball past her. She didn't get a break but won."

Responded Ms. King, "This is a culmination of nineteen years of tennis for me. I've wanted to change the sport, and tonight a lot of non-tennis people saw the sport for the first time." The impact of the match was shown soon after by the increased crowds that came out to watch women's tournament play. As Billie Jean said, looking over one such audience, "Women's tennis has come a long way since I used to be the warm-up show for men's tennis."

5

ANNE HENNING
Speed Skating

Suburban Northbrook, Illinois, doesn't look much different from any other growing town on the outskirts of a major midwestern city. Neither its name nor that of Allis, Wisconsin, a little to the north just over the state border, rings many bells with most people. But to skating fans the world over, these towns are famous. Northbrook has been the source of almost all U.S. world-class speed skaters in recent years, and its products include such great women performers as Diane Holum, Leah Poulos and a quiet, blue-eyed youngster named Anne Henning who became known as the world's fastest woman skater in the early 1970s.

It's surprising in a country the size of the United States to find one town supplying the majority of athletes who help put the nation on the map in one field of sports. One reason given for this state of affairs is the presence of the *only* Olympic-size skating rink in all of the United States in Allis, Wisconsin. The children of Northbrook are among the few in the country who can practice under conditions like those encountered in international skating matches. However, to do this they have to travel eighty or ninety miles round trip each day that they want to use the Allis rink. There are other towns in the region that one would think could be the source of good skating prospects. But the fact remains that only Northbrook proved to have not one but literally dozens of boys and girls with both natural talent and the competitive desire.

One other reason, perhaps the key one, was Ed Rudolph. A one-time world-class skater, he moved to Northbrook in his early twenties in the mid-1930s and started a landscaping business. The business prospered and gave him the financial stability that let him devote his leisure hours to skating and, in time, to coaching a local speed-skating program. This project was sponsored by the parks department, of which Ed became commissioner in the 1960s. Many Northbrook parents enrolled their children in the program, and Rudolph's seasoned eye was always peeled for exceptional ability.

Most children in the area came to skating naturally during the winter months as did their peer group in all the places where waterways froze over and the winter climate had plenty of nip in it. Anne Henning's parents both enjoyed skating and got their daughter a pair of learner's skates in 1960 when she was four. Little Anne took her share of spills, but over the next couple of years she developed a sense of balance and had moved up to single-runner skates by the time she entered elementary school.

Anne proved to have fine co-ordination and a flair

for all kinds of sports. She was a powerful swimmer before she was in her teens, and also proved adept at throwing and batting a baseball. Besides continuing her ice skating, she developed prowess as a skier, beginning on the gentle slopes of the local hills, and trying more difficult ones as time went on.

But the turning point came in 1966 when she joined the Northbrook speed-skating program. She had spent many hours then and in previous winters frolicking on the ice, either frozen ponds in the park or at local skating rinks, with her parents or friends. By the time she was nine, she could handle herself well on skates and her parents posed no objections to her going into Ed Rudolph's class the next year.

It took only a few sessions for her to catch Rudolph's attention. As he watched the easy grace with which this little girl with the blondish, flowing hair moved across the glistening ice surface, he could tell that she had great potential. He told a reporter some years later, "She was a genius on skates. When I first saw her, I saw nothing but gold medals dancing before my eyes. She was born for it."

He sought both Anne's and her parents' approval for the detailed training program needed to prepare her for major competition. He pointed out she would have to devote countless hours to the sport and it would have to be a constant, week-in, week-out effort. He stated his belief Anne could eventually go to the top of the field. He cautioned that in speed skating the rewards were mainly in the form of self-satisfaction and the opportunity to travel to many parts of the world and meet a wide range of people.

Anne's parents were not fanatics about success in sports. They were in moderately comfortable circumstances—Bill Henning had a good reputation as a hospital consultant and Joanne Henning taught nursery school. They understood, though, that they would have to invest money in Anne's career for equipment and training, but they were willing to do it as long as Anne was interested. As Bill told *Sports Illustrated*, ". . . it was no huge debate. This sort of thing doesn't need to create a world crisis. There was no compulsion about it, we just want Annie to do it only as long as she enjoys it. If she needs our support, we're here to give it. This is sport—not a lifetime career."

There wasn't any problem as far as Anne was concerned. She loved skating and she didn't mind spending more time on it than her friends did. Under Rudolph's direction, she went through a regular routine of developing her wind and endurance and streamlining her skating form for maximum efficiency. Every day after school she rushed to the rink to join the others in the group in limbering-up exercises followed by an almost endless round of skating action. Sometimes the skaters just swept around the rink to practice the proper position—crouched low over the ice with one hand swinging free and the other held behind the back. Sometimes Rudolph asked them to do sprints against the clock to develop speed and the ability to work easily under pressure. Sometimes some were paired against each other in practice heats.

As often as possible, the most talented members were ferried to Allis where the long oval course duplicated the layout of the centers of speed skating in cities and towns around the world. The program they followed was very different from that followed by the relative handful of other speed-skating hopefuls in other parts of the country. They had to learn to race the way their international opponents raced, the approach used in all world championships. This required overcoming the tendency to think of direct competition against a number of other racers. World standards demanded the ability to race unseen opponents because the deciding factor isn't who comes in first in a particular race but which of several skaters covers the distance in the fastest time.

In international skating, competitors only race in pairs. One skater could beat his or her immediate opponent by a wide margin, yet have a time that would only lead to a 4, 5, or worse placing overall. Thus, a successful skater must learn his or her capabilities and must be able to pace herself to achieve just the right level of movement. In effect, a speed skater must have an imaginary clock in her head, born of hours of practice plus competitive experience, that signals when she is hitting the right pace for a particular distance and permits her to keep up that pace at a steady rate. For Anne, Dianne, Leah and the other American hopefuls, it required developing tremendous concentration, something retained only through year-round workouts.

Adding to their need for a single-minded attention to skating skills during the winter months was the requirement to shut out the depressing conditions of the Allis rink in the wintertime. The oval is located on the Milwaukee Fair Grounds near the famed football town of Green Bay. During winter months, it gives an impression of desolation and loneliness marked by empty barns and ice-encrusted stands. The skaters must make their way around the rink in weather often gray and overcast. Chill winds wail and moan across the still farmlands most of the day.

But Anne and the other girls maintained their cheerfulness and intensity for one season after another as they expanded their knowledge under the coach's firm direction. Anne was only a novice when Dianne Holum and some of the more experienced skaters from Northbrook represented the United States at the 1968 Olympic Games in Grenoble, France. She joined in the welcome for Dianne, who returned with a silver medal in the 500 meters and an unexpected bronze in the 1,000. Experts forecast possible gold medals for Holum in both races four years later, but both Dianne and Ed Rudolph were aware she might be sharing honors with Anne by then.

By the end of the '60s, both Dianne and Anne were showing better and better form and consistency. Dianne placed high in world class meets at home and abroad, and Anne achieved steadily faster times in local races. By mid-1970, Rudolph felt Anne was ready for bigger things and added Anne's name to those who would enter major European skating events in the winter of 1970–71. Anne, Dianne and Leah all went across the seas in the fall to train for a month on the much better rinks of Europe with the advice of some of the great coaches from the area, such as Holland's Leen Pfrommer.

In November, Anne had her first chance before

one of the typical large and enthusiastic crowds that watched skating races in Europe, a far cry from the meager turnouts for the occasional meets back home. Not all the top European stars were at the event in Inzell in the German Alps, but there were enough of the good ones to strongly test fifteen-year-old Anne. She was a virtual unknown when she took her place at the starting line in one of two well-marked lanes. After she had flashed around the silvery surface in the 500-meter sprint, she was obscure no longer. The onlookers, most of them well versed in the fine points of the sport, quickly noted her strong, sure skating strokes and sensed that she was far from an ordinary athlete. The applause and shouts crescendoed as she clearly outclassed her opponent and chalked up a fantastic 43.7 seconds.

Her time barely missed equaling the world record held by Russian expert Tatiana Sidorva. Rudolph happily told reporters he was certain Anne was the world's fastest, and forecast she would prove it at the speed-skating championships in Helsinki, Finland, in early 1971. His view, of course, was broader than that. Both he and Anne already were thinking about the chance for gold at the 1972 Olympic Winter Games, slated for Sapporo, Japan, a year later.

The girls were back in Northbrook during December and early January, but as the Helsinki meet neared, Rudolph had his team fly to Oslo, Norway, for two weeks of practice. The goal was to get good workouts in well-prepared facilities and also to get everyone used to the local time, which was eight hours different from that back home.

Though there were ten other nations from both the Communist and non-Communist world present, the teen-agers from America got the lion's share of attention when they arrived in the Finnish capital. Local fans were impressed by their appearance and the threat they held for the more-established stars from Russia and Holland. Large crowds turned out to watch them try the ice of the Helsinki stadium and reporters from European papers and TV sought to interview them at every opportunity. All of this did little to reduce the pressure. Rudolph did his best to get the girls to take it all in stride, telling them to do their best, win or lose.

The condition of the ice worried the U.S. team. The temperature, while far from warm, wasn't quite low enough for the rink to freeze properly and the constant tread of newsmen across it left ruts and dirt smudges that maintenance crews worked long and hard to patch up. A new world record seemed out of reach. Rudolph worried that the rink's poor condition might work against the less-experienced skaters like Anne.

When the 500 got underway, Russia's Ludmila Tatova set the standard with an excellent 45.8 seconds. Dianne Holum was the first U.S. entry to skate and was thought to be the prime hope for a victory. But the ice was dirty and hard to get traction and Dianne ended with a disappointing 48.3. The U.S. challenge seemed to have lost, for few thought Anne, one of the youngest skaters in international competition, was ready yet for this kind of racing. However, the small-seeming blue-clad figure soon changed all that as she shot from the starting line with skates flashing and her free arm swinging back and forth in perfect pendulum rhythm. As she changed lanes at the halfway point, many eyes glanced at stopwatches and realized she was hitting the best time yet. Seconds later she was across the finish line to a roar of approval that accurately foretold an official time of 44.6. No one else bettered it and Anne had the first U.S. gold medal in world-class women's racing in many years.

Dianne came back to take a gold in the 1,000 and a bronze in the 1,500. Overall, she placed fourth and missed a bronze by only 118/1,000 of a point. The outlook for Sapporo seemed brighter than ever for the United States.

Still, the girls and their mentors knew the Olympics were a long way off and much could happen in between. They had to keep up their training and do everything that could be done to refine their talents even beyond the levels of Helsinki. The schedule called for entering as many meets as possible for the rest of '71 to gain poise and self-confidence under strain and to practice, practice, practice. Back in the United States there was even less room for parties, entertainment or other "frivolities" than before. But with the attraction of Olympic gold on the horizon, no one minded the extra work. During the summer, the girls went to the rink in the evening to avoid the warmer midday temperatures, but they managed to get in four, five or more hours of skating almost every day of the year.

They worked on slight changes in technique—the position of their body to reduce air resistance or the precise sharpening of their skate blades—to coax an added tenth or thousandth of a second improvement in time. Rudolph studied movies of their performances to try to detect ways of doing this. The months went by and the training intensified as the time neared for the trip to the Orient.

One thing was certain when Anne and the rest got their first look at the Olympic rink. With help from the sometimes fickle winter weather, it would be about as fine a course as could be desired. Japanese crews worked ceaselessly to polish the surface to a glasslike consistency in which the snow-capped mountains around the stadium were sharply reflected. The girls found the rink to their liking and looked forward eagerly to each day's workout.

But as the time for the 500 came close, with the finest speed skaters in the world due to take part, the impact of the event caught up with Anne. The night before, she found she could hardly take a bite of supper. She stayed in her room and listened to music on a tape recorder by the light of a single candle as she fought to ignore an occasional sinking feeling in her stomach. Somehow she got to sleep and was fatalistically more at ease as she entered the jammed stadium in the morning. The crowd was one of the largest she'd ever seen for a skating race; tens of thousands of people took up every inch of the low-lying, single-tiered oval. Among the thousands of eyes riveted on her, she also knew, would be those of many Northbrook residents, including her parents, who had made the long trip to root their girls home.

The early pairs began the action to the ringing support of the crowd. However, their times didn't seem to indicate any great advantage over Anne. To the onlookers, the races went by fast enough, but for Anne and Ed Rudolph, the second hand seemed to crawl until her pairing, with Canada's Sylvia Burka, was called out. Anne had drawn the outside lane for the first half of the race, normally a slightly slower lane because the distance a skater had to cover was a little more than when the inside lane was used. The crossover at the halfway point, of course, was used to even up things. Soon Anne and Sylvia were crouched at the starting line as the starting gun went up. The signal came and both girls sped into the track as the crowd found its voice. As they streaked around the oval, Anne was setting a demanding pace, so fast that she was even with her rival where usually the outer lane skater is a few lengths behind. Closer and closer the girls came to the crossover, matching stride for stride, but there was a danger coming up. As Burka headed for the outer lane, it was crucial that she synchronize her lane shift with the fast-moving Henning.

The two got to that point with Anne holding a lead, which meant that Burka by international rules was supposed to give way and let her go first. The crowd gasped as they realized the Canadian was continuing to move without changing speed. Anne tried to get through, but Burka blocked her way. For a moment it seemed they might collide. At the last second, Anne rose up from her crouch and braked herself with one skate. For ten meters she had to back off before resuming her position and setting off in pursuit of her opponent. Amazingly, she steadily narrowed the gap. The crowd egged her on with every ounce of vocal strength they could muster. To a resounding roar of support, Anne blazed past the line in a winning time of 43.73, almost enough to set a world's record.

The judges hastily conferred, then announced Burka was disqualified for failing to yield. The crowd cheered wildly at the announcement, then shouted even more lustily when it was announced that Anne had been offered a second run by herself after all entrants had raced, to make up for the foul.

For a time, some wondered whether Anne would bother. Skater after skater tried to better her time and failed. As result after result went up on the electronically operated board, the visitors from Northbrook smiled broadly. No one was coming even close to Anne. When the last pairing finished, she was indisputably the gold medal winner.

But Anne still stepped out to the line to claim her penalty run. The crowd hunched forward expectantly as the blue-clad figure with the white-edged red "U.S.A." on her uniform slid into place. The starter signaled get ready, held his gun high, paused, then pulled the trigger. Hair streaming behind, her skates flashing in the bright wintry sun, Anne was poetry in motion as she began her second quest. Legs pumping rhythmically, body tucked in for minimum wind resistance she picked up speed, hit the right level and held it. Fans clapped in unison, forgot usual Japanese decorum to send peals of sound volleying across the hills and dells of the Sapporo countryside to urge her on. Her clocking at the crossover was tenths ahead of her first run. Without slackening speed, she swept into the other lane and continued to streak toward the finish line. Around the world, countless eyes watched the small figure with the bright red cap head into the home stretch. In rooms across the world, individuals shouted to the four walls as Anne crossed the line in what the unofficial clock on the corner of the screen indicated was a possible world-beating time.

Soon it was official. Anne had won the gold medal not once, but twice in the same day, the second time in 43.3 seconds. As Rudolph had predicted, she was the fastest woman on skates.

6

ROBYN SMITH
Horse Racing, Jockey

The field of maiden three-year-olds came thundering into the clubhouse turn at fabled Santa Anita Race Track bunched closely together. Jockey Angel Santiago on Big Red Rambler briefly saw an opening and headed out toward the rail. But another horse, Ennius, ridden by Fernando Toro, was coming up fast and had to swerve rapidly to avoid a collision. As it did, it forced a third horse, Faithville Rider, right up against the rail.

A yell of dismay burst from the throats of thousands of spectators as Faithville Rider slipped and fell, hurling its slim rider to the ground. As the shrill wail of an ambulance siren split the air, the form lay still for an instant, then quickly got up and started to walk away. The ambulance came alongside and motioned the rider to get in back, but the rider, ramrod straight, would not agree. It took all the powers of persuasion the driver could muster to convince the jockey to at least get in the front seat for a ride to the stands.

The iron will, the refusal to give in to the odds or to the pain of a fall that could have caused serious injury was characteristic of this jockey. For this super-star of the "Sport of Kings" was a girl named Robyn Smith who had determined to prove that her sex could challenge the greatest male riders on even terms and win. The rousing cheers from the crowded stands as she determinedly stepped from the ambulance and strode away quickly to the dressing room demonstrated she had already proved her point.

Robyn had almost literally come from nowhere to star billing in racing in only a few years. Before 1968, there is no evidence she had ever spent much time on a horse, but by 1969, she was appearing at the major tracks in the country and maintaining a good share of winners among the mounts she was given. To do this, she had discarded every vestige of her earlier life and had created an aura of mystery about it. She said little about her first twenty-two or twenty-three years, and what she did tell interviewers only added to the confusion. It seemed certain that her original name wasn't Robyn Smith and her claim to have been born in San Francisco was hard to verify. It seemed likely that she was born in 1944, although it was always possible she was a year or two older, or younger.

But a bit of her previous history could be detected, enough to show that Robyn had sacrificed a great deal to carry the banner of women forward in sports. She had looked, at one time, the image of the Hollywood starlet. One thing known about her was that she had been in the movie capital for a number of years where she studied at the Columbia Studio's acting workshop. A number of film executives who knew her then be-lieved she could have gone on to greatness as an actress, a path millions of women would give their eyeteeth to follow.

But Robyn had a strong urge to avoid the obvious. She wanted to achieve, but in her own way. The first stirrings of other objectives came after she met horse trainer Bruce Headley. He took her to the stables and showed her some of his charges. Robyn was impressed with the beauty and grace of the animals and found a certain peace and happiness in being with them. Before long, she had gained Headley's approval to work the horses in the gray hours of dawn. She could do this and still make her acting classes later in the day.

It was a learning experience for both Robyn and the horses. As she told a *Sports Illustrated* reporter, "The horses weren't so scared, but boy, I was. Invariably they'd run away with me, but it was dark in the morning that time of the year and Headley couldn't see. One day, when it got lighter in the morning, he said, 'Gee, you don't gallop real good, do you?'"

However, Robyn had risen to the new challenge. She doggedly kept working to improve her riding skills. It was no easy task, even though it was apparent she had been born with natural athletic ability. Most jockeys start learning their trade in early youth. Some work as exercise boys or ride horses in rural areas before they're in their teens. At Robyn's relatively advanced age of twenty-three it was hard to gain the automatic reflexes so vital to any physical activity. It required twice as much concentration and effort to make up for lost time. Robyn had made up her mind she could—and would—do it. She spent more and more hours around local tracks and riding facilities studying other riders, finding out all she could about horses and their habits. And she spent many hours in the saddle, taking directions from Headley and other experts, finding out how to sit properly, how to use the reins, how to apply the whip.

People began to talk about her dedication and gradually, somewhat in awe, of her growing ability. However, few of the male onlookers would have taken any bets on her chances for making it as a jockey. Though there were a few rumblings about women's rights in the field and attempts by some women riders in some parts of the country to enter the sport, not many men took it seriously. It was a rugged, demanding job requiring physical strength, fearlessness and patience. How could a slight, demure-looking girl like Robyn make her way against such obstacles?

Outward appearances, as the few who were close to Robyn knew, could be very deceiving. Anyone who could apply herself as she did could keep pecking away at the artificial walls set up by the racing powers and could provide the persistence needed to take advantage of any chink in the edifice. For Robyn, the first opening showed in March 1969 when word of her growing proficiency reached Kjell Qvale, a member of the board of directors of Golden Gate Park near San Francisco. It was, plain and simple, mainly a publicity gimmick. With the growing clamor for women's rights, racing officials had agreed that girls could get jockey's licenses. Qvale figured having a woman rider would attract attention to his track. Robyn got the bid, accepted and with considerable fanfare from the local press, took part in her first official race on April 5.

The horse wasn't the best in the world and Robyn still had many rough edges as a jockey. So the pairing finished out of the money. The track was happy with the notice it got, though, and Robyn was well satisfied because it brought her the all-important license as an accredited rider.

She went back to her training grind, intensifying it even more. She read all the books she could find about horses and horse racing, crediting one written by hall-of-fame jockey Eddie Arcaro with giving her much of the technique she developed in handling her mounts. Much of her program was devoted to exercising; long runs every morning, special routines to impart the strength of steel wires to her muscles. And along with this came a near starvation diet. Keeping one's weight down is something most women of today live with all their lives, but for a jockey it's not just a matter of pride, but a crucial necessity. A few pounds of extra weight on a horse can make the difference between an easy win and finishing out of the money. The average jockey starts with an advantage. He is usually short, (5 feet or less) and small boned.

Robyn came to the sport with, if anything, slightly bigger proportions than most women. Her 5-foot, 7-inch height is certainly normal for her sex, and her build, typically, would have a healthy weight of 125–30 pounds. To compete with regular jockeys, Robyn had to cut her weight by twenty pounds or more—and keep it there. It meant cutting way down on food and avoiding fancy restaurants or parties where a little bit of rich entree or dessert could cause immediate results on the weighing scale.

All of this Robyn observed religiously. And, as 1969

went by, she persevered at complementing that training with experience in actual races. It was tough going, for men still didn't like the idea of competing directly with a woman. The big stables avoided her, but she managed to race here and there in small-time events at county fairs. It paid off in another way. At one local race, she met a New York trainer named Buddy Jacobson. Impressed with her potential, he suggested she come East with him to try to get some races at the big-time tracks. She agreed, though soon after she arrived in New York the two went different ways. No one knew her and she made the rounds of stables, begging for a chance for even one mount to prove herself.

Trainers were usually kind, but firm. They listened, then allowed that they already had a rider. As the days went by, the nest egg of money Robyn had brought began to dwindle. It was late fall by then and the race dates were coming to an end. Going from barn to barn, Robyn felt increasingly desperate as the preparations for movement to southern tracks became increasingly apparent. She had exhausted all her possibilities, but she began all over again. In a driving rainstorm she approached the barn of trainer Frank Wright, her hair matted down and water soaking into every stitch of clothing. Her forlorn-looking figure made Wright reconsider an earlier turndown. He had used girls to exercise his horses in the past and was not unsympathetic to their aspirations.

He agreed to find a horse for her before the season ended. Soon after, he got one client, a Detroit dentist, to let Robyn ride a horse named Exotic Bird. The animal wasn't very exotic. It rarely even placed in the first three finishers and usually ended up last. But for Robyn it was a glimmer of hope. She excitedly got ready for her first race at Aqueduct, a proud name in horse-racing annals, one of the top ten tracks in the United States.

The date was December 5, 1969, when Robyn rode her charge into the starting gates. She whispered in the horse's ear and gentled it as the handlers checked the horse's position behind the narrow padded barrier. The starter got the signal that all entries were in place and ready; he hit the button that swung the gates open. Eight gleaming mounts, Robyn's among them, flashed from the spidery metal framework, their hooves kicking up sprays of dirt behind. From the beginning, Exotic Bird remained in the thick of things. Crouched low over the horse's neck, Robyn urged him on, hearing the thunder of straining bodies around her as they went past the quarter pole, then the halfway mark. As they neared the head of the home stretch, Exotic Bird was still hanging in there moving with three others a few strides behind the leaders. The two front runners opened noticeable distance between them and the pack, but the fight for third and a share of the prize money was intense. As the first and second place horses headed for the line, Robyn gave Exotic Bird the whip and fought to edge out her two competitors. One of them slipped back and now it was Robyn and one other rival bearing down on the final few lengths neck and neck. To the screams of delirious fans, the two swept across the line so close the human eye couldn't tell the leader. Minutes later, the judges examined a photo and decreed Robyn's horse had lost by a nose.

Still, it was a notable achievement, the best performance ever for Exotic Bird. To Frank Wright and other trainers, it was obvious that Robyn was a pro. As he told Frank Deford of *Sports Illustrated,* "There's a mechanics in all sports and a lot of people pick that up. But beyond that, there's a naturalness that can't be learned. In riding, when someone has that, we just say that horses run for him. You can't see it in specific style or technique. You just find it out. . . . Well, horses run for Robyn, and you could sense that right away. . . . Trainers accepted Robyn long before owners."

Wright kept providing Robyn with occasional mounts as the months went by. Then Robyn got even more recognition when Wright's opinion was seconded by the head of one of the most respected racing tables, Allen Jerkens of Hobeau Farm. Once Jerkens started to assign Robyn some of his well-groomed, fleet horses, she was considered to have arrived as a rider of first-class rank.

From then on, Robyn was listened to when she sought the chance to ride, and she became a familiar figure to track fans at major meets around the country in the 1970s. But not as familiar as Robyn deserved. She still had to work twice as hard as other top-flight jockeys even to get a respectable number of rides. For the first few years of the 1970s, while other jockeys of her experience and caliber might get a thousand or more rides a year, Robyn was lucky to get close to a hundred. Her performance on the horses she did get to ride was usually hard to fault. She almost always got more out of a horse than its previous record indicated it was capable of. And given a superior mount, she almost always turned in a superior race. From 1970–74, she maintained a winning percentage of 18–20 per cent of all her races, an achievement matched by few male opponents.

And slowly, exasperatingly slowly, her chances to ride went up too. From her few rides of 1969, the total went to over sixty in 1970, a little over a hundred in 1971 and then in the hundreds in 1972. She maintained her ratio of victories in 1972 even though racing authorities recognized her increased status by removing her "apprentice allowance" in January of that year.

The apprentice allowance is an advantage in weight given an inexperienced rider, usually around five pounds. This is done by reducing the extra "handicap" weight placed on horses to even up the chance of slower horses competing against more talented rivals. If a jockey does not improve his or her skills markedly by the time this advantage is taken away, the result generally is a lower winning average. In Robyn's case, she improved her ability to such an extent that it awed many male riders. Those who watched her in 1972 estimated she was anywhere from 60–80 per cent better in all aspects of riding except perhaps handling her whip, than the year before.

Her obvious expertise won her a position as regular rider for one of the foremost owners of racing tables, Alfred Gwynne Vanderbilt. Sporting his silks in the 1972 spring meeting at Aqueduct, she made many trips to the winner's circle. Even with this, she received only half the mounts that male riders did during the series. Despite this, she won 20 per cent of her races, a feat that made her number seven winning jockey of the meet.

In the mid-1970s, she edged closer to full acceptance. All the prestige tracks and events were open to her now. Other trainers sought her out during periods when, for one reason or another, she was not riding regularly for Vanderbilt. She followed the racing season to Florida, California, Kentucky for the legendary Derby, Maryland for the great races at Pimlico (including one that formed part of the "Triple Crown"), Belmont, Aqueduct and Saratoga in New York. At Santa Anita, where she had made her first halting attempts at riding a few years before, she sometimes rode three or four horses in a single day, breezing past the finish line in front on many occasions.

Her breakthrough cleared the way for others. People like Cheryl White, a petite black jockey who began making the circuit of small tracks as a teen-ager in the early '70s. Before long, she was riding at some of the big tracks too, sometimes challenging Robyn herself as she did at Atlantic City in 1971. By 1972, Cheryl proved she was moving ahead when she rode Heliamber, the horse Robyn had mounted in the Boots and Bows Purse the year before, and won going away.

For Robyn still kept the drive to excel in the mid-1970s. In a sport where top riders like Willie Shoemaker, Arcaro and the like are often still dominating the field in their forties, she had a long road ahead if she wanted to pursue it. And by all indicators, she meant to do just that until some of the most glittering awards were within reach, perhaps a victory in the

Kentucky Derby or even a shot at the pinnacle of the Triple Crown.

Whatever the future, by the mid-'70s Robyn had attained something many would envy her for—a certain peace of mind. She had come to love horses and valued being with them perhaps more than the companionship of other human beings. And with her attainments, she could indulge this desire to the fullest. For someone who saw her in the morning, leading a glistening four-footed friend out to graze, it was a reward in itself to see the glow of happiness, of true personal freedom radiant on her face.

7

WYOMIA TYUS
SIMBURG
Track

In the early spring of 1974, the infant professional track program came of age. In its first nationally televised outdoor meet from El Paso, Texas, it treated a huge viewing audience to a series of brilliant performances. Steve Smith soared to breathtaking heights in the pole vault; the great John Carlos flashed to victory with excellent times in the 100- and 220-yard dashes; and Wyomia Tyus Simburg blazed a time of 10.3 in the women's 100, equaling the fastest time for that distance in her career.

For both Wyomia and the organizers of pro track, the International Track Association (ITA), it was sweet vindication. When the ITA announced it would bring "play-for-pay" to the world of track and field, many sports writers and track experts expressed doubts. It wouldn't work, they said; the best performances would still be made in amateur meets, and who'd want to see second best. True, they agreed, the ITA could get some famous names, like the illustrious Jim Ryun

or lure former stars like Wyomia Tyus from retire-
ment. It might draw fans for a while, but the question
remained, could the one-time headliners live up to
their earlier reputations? If this happened, fans might
continue to come in large numbers, providing the cash
rewards that would make amateur stars want to join
the pro track tour and provide the basis for future
growth. Without it, the whole idea would pass into
history.

In the case of Wyomia Tyus Simburg, it seemed a
particularly strong argument. When she agreed to take
part in the first ITA meet in 1973, she had not trained
for five years. She had accomplished much in the
1960s, establishing herself as one of the world's all-
time great sprinters. But when she reached the pinnacle of her amateur career in the '68 Olympics, she
had decided it was time to step down from the training grind and live a more normal life. The five-year
lapse from then to 1973, said the naysayers, was too
big for her to come back.

However, Wyomia wasn't pessimistic. She could look
back on an athletic career that had often progressed
in ways that had surprised her as much as track-wise
coaches. She knew she had great natural ability—her
body seemed so well co-ordinated for running that
she often achieved notable successes under training
conditions that would have ruined the chances of other
athletes. She had learned it was always worth trying.
The results might come out better than seemed possible.

As a girl growing up on a dairy farm in Griffin,
Georgia, where she was born on August 29, 1945, she

paid little heed to organized sports. Until the family house burned down and they moved to the small town nearby, Wyomia and her brothers roamed freely through the rural Georgia countryside. In a way, this was a form of preparation. She recalls, "I grew up with three brothers and I had to keep up with them a lot or run away from them a lot. I guess it helped me decide to take part later when we had field days in junior high school. When I'd do that, people would say, 'You're pretty fast' and I'd mumble a short 'OK.' But after a while I began to run with the girls' team. We didn't compete in anything special, just local meets in Georgia."

Wyomia didn't win all the time, but she did reasonably well and was considered one of the top runners on her team. She enjoyed running, but didn't give too much thought to what she would do in later years. Then the track coach of Tennessee State University, Edward Temple, who had developed some of the U.S.'s world-class women runners of the 1950s and early '60s, was in Georgia and saw Wyomia take part in a state meet. His experienced eye detected the great potential of her relaxed, flowing style. "After the race," says Wyomia, "he came up to me and complimented me on my effort. He told me he had a summer program at Tennessee State for junior high and high school runners, and if I took part and did well, I might get an athletic scholarship."

Wyomia eagerly accepted the offer. From then on, most of her teen-age summer months were spent in Nashville on the Tennessee State campus where she began to follow a regular instruction program. There wasn't much effort to change her style; a good runner tends to be born, not made. But the need to strengthen the body muscles to develop strong breathing is another matter. Wyomia started the routine of long exercise periods and a daily program of practice runs over a variety of distances so familiar to athletes.

Her new mentor seemed to have a quiet confidence in his young charge, but Wyomia had some self-doubts. Tennessee State hadn't become a power in track by accident. The staff sought out top talent, and as it turned out such champions as Wilma Rudolph, many promising runners sought it out. "That first summer," Wilma notes, "I suddenly found myself in really top competition. It always seemed there were girls faster than me taking part."

After completing her junior year in Griffin High School, Wyomia returned for a second summer at Tennessee State in 1963. The girls working out on campus still looked like rugged competition, but once the track meets began, all her fears faded away. Wyomia had grown taller, reaching a well-proportioned 5 feet, 7 inches, and demonstrated a steadily maturing style. By midsummer, she was in top form, easily winning time trials from teammates in her age bracket. As the days went by—warm, lazy ones for most teenagers but full of perspiring effort for Wyomia—she began to gain the rewards of her dedication. She became one of the nation's outstanding young performers in the sprints, setting fast times in the 50-, 75- and 100-yard dashes in AAU competition. Before she returned for her senior year in high school, she went to

California and raced to victory in the 100-yard dash in the girls' division nationals.

The following year, scholarship in hand, she enrolled in Tennessee State. As did most track hopefuls, she went out for cross country in the fall. Cross country, a sport in which competitors race each other over unprepared courses usually involving stretches through parks or rugged back-country areas, demands building up a great deal of stamina. Day after day between meets, Wyomia had to run six long miles, sometimes in addition to a prescribed number of short-distance practice laps. Although it's wearing, it is considered fine conditioning for the track season.

The cross-country season lasts until fall and, at most schools where track is emphasized, is followed by daily workouts leading up to the track season in late winter or early spring. Amazingly, in Wyomia's case, each year there was a gap in her workouts. "After the last cross-country race in November, we didn't put on sneakers until January. It was cold outside, usually with snow on the ground, and you couldn't use the track. We couldn't use the gym because the basketball team had it. We could start doing some indoor exercising sometime in January, but we didn't get outside until March."

When Wyomia came off this winter rest period during her first year at Tennessee State, it was into a season that had Olympic gold as a lure for many sprinters. Even as she joined such more experienced college runners as Edith Maguire, in early workouts, Wyomia gave little thought to the games of late summer slated to be held in far-off Japan. "I was young and a newcomer and there were people out there already being compared to Wilma Rudolph, who'd come from our campus, to star in the Olympics. I had plenty to do just getting in shape for regular meets."

The schedule began with some exercises and laps around the gym, finally relinquished by the basketball team. It expanded as the girls finally got the chance for outdoor practice. "In a typical week on the track we'd start with 3–5 330s on Mondays, running about half to three-quarter speed. On Tuesdays and Thursdays we worked on starts; we'd go over the right way to get down and leave the starting blocks, and maybe we'd try some all-out dashes. On Thursdays the sprinters did a series of flying 100s—that is, we'd go into them from a running start. On Fridays we had time trials in the 220s."

Most team members kept right on working on weekends. Wyomia, as she often did, defied tradition. "I feel you need some time for your body to recuperate. I believe if you do everything you should five days in the week, you won't be hurt by a few days off." Most experts would say a few days off had to take a little off timing and co-ordination. Often, though, for a truly great athlete, the rules don't seem to apply as rigorously. Mark Spitz's unequaled accomplishments in the '72 Olympics is an example. It's generally agreed that for a swimmer the less hair on the body the less frictional resistance will be met from the water. But while his rivals often had shaven heads and bodies, Spitz sported long hair and a mustache, which didn't prevent him from winning seven gold medals in seven tries.

When track season began it looked briefly as if the

traditionalists might be right. Wyomia didn't do badly, but she wasn't all-winning. However, she points out, "I've always been a slow starter." By midseason things were going better and Wyomia did well enough to be entered in the Olympic trials. "I didn't think of it as more than a chance for more experience. Most people thought Edna Maguire could be another Wilma Rudolph. No one paid too much attention to me. My coach said he thought my year would be 1968. He told me, 'If you make the team, great, but if not, there's plenty of time left.'

"So I went into it without worrying. I did well in the first heats in the 100-meter dash. The coach told me I had a good chance to make it to the finals. I won each heat and when I got ready for the final one he was getting excited. 'You really have a chance to make the team,' he said. I didn't win, but I placed in the top three and that was good enough for a ticket to Japan. I was very happy to go. It was a nice way to go because there wasn't that much pressure then. I hadn't been picked to win and I'd come farther than everyone expected, including myself. Whatever I did in the Olympics was a bonus."

Before the packed stands in the stadium built just for the '64 games, young Ms. Tyus did very well indeed. She didn't take first in all the heats, but always did well enough to qualify for the next round of the eliminations. Then it was the finals and she found herself loosening up in the starting blocks along with the finest female sprinters in the world. When the gun went off, all the girls seemed to leave as one and for the first 10–15 meters, it was hard to tell who was ahead. Then Wyomia took charge, holding a slim lead over several other contenders and finally leaning into the tape in first place. In her first try, she had won it all and could proudly display the heavy gold medal with the five interconnected rings imprinted on it. There were some months of relaxation, but come the fall of 1964 she was back at it again, running the usual six miles a day practice course for cross country. Now she was a celebrity and more people than usual turned out to watch the lightly attended cross-country races. In the spring and summer, she was featured at many major track meets across the country, a pattern repeated as she continued her years at Tennessee State.

When 1968 rolled around, it was a foregone conclusion Wyomia would be a contender for the Olympic team. Unlike 1964, the pressure was on. She could feel the anxieties that came from being in the spotlight, knowing full well that there were outstanding challengers coming along, such as Margaret Bailes and Barbara Ferrell. As the months went by, she was running as well as she ever had in regular meets. Still, in the AAU championships in Denver, Colorado, she placed second in the 100 behind Margaret Bailes. Some experts wondered if this was a portent for the Mexico City games. No one, man or woman, had ever won two consecutive gold medals in the 100 meters.

"The Olympic trials were held in Walnut, California," Wyomia recalls, "and I was facing Margaret Bailes, Barbara Ferrell and several other great sprinters. But when race time came I was ready and won the 100. I also placed in the 220 meter finals and made the sprint relay team. One of the more difficult phases was the training schedule at Los Alamos, New Mexico. The people there were wonderful, really nice, but the exercises and the practice we went through to get the squad adapted to running at altitude really took a lot out of you. (Mexico City is at an altitude of over a mile above sea level and the air is much thinner than at the usual locations of athletic competitions.) It was good conditioning, but actually I feel it was more important for those in longer races. Sprinters run a short distance and altitude doesn't affect them too much."

It was still one of the most exciting times in Wyomia's life when the team took up quarters in Mexico City in late summer. She tried not to think of the 100-meter "repeat jinx" and concentrated on practicing her starts, an area in which she knew she could improve. When the heats began, if she was worrying it wasn't evident to the huge crowds that jammed the track and field stadium. She went through the preliminaries without any obvious strain, as did both other U.S. 100-meter stars, Barbara Ferrell and Margaret Bailes. When the finals were at hand, the threesome was joined at the starting line by a strong international field that included Chi Cheng, representing Taiwan; Raelene Boyle of Australia; Miguelina Cobian of Cuba; Irena Kirszenstein of Poland; and Dianne Burge of Australia.

As Wyomia watched an official hammer in the nails holding the metal starting blocks in place, she was vaguely aware of the buzz of the crowd and the presence of her challengers. "I can't remember anything unusual passing through my mind. I kept thinking 'I'll be glad when it's over with.' I guess I was aware I was on the verge of doing something that had never been done before, but I tried not to consider success or failure."

The starter watched the girls limber up and checked to make sure the officials monitoring the finish were ready at the other end of the course. Finally he signaled the runners to move into the blocks. Nine forms assumed the kneeling position, heads cocked for the starter's commands. The call came out, "get ready," and some of the girls kicked a leg in the air to loosen the muscles or took a hand from the ground and waved it as if to increase the circulation. To the competitors the seconds dragged out until "get set" rang out. Perspiration beads dotted their faces; sweat moistened their track clothes as they tensed for the third, all important command. It came at last—"go"— and the crouching bodies sprang forward and sent little puffs of dust into the air from their swiftly moving feet.

Though the crowd sent a tremendous volley of sound into the air, Wyomia was hardly conscious of it. She had no time to look right or left, but stared at the rapidly diminishing stretch of brown, white-lined surface between her and the thin white tape. Her teammates kept pace with her most of the way as did some of the others, but she matched them with powerful strides and then drew to the front to flash past the timers in first place for the second time in four years. She was clocked in 11.0, a record at the time, and better than her 11.2 mark in the '64 Games.

She stood alone on the victory stand's top rung a

little later to watch the U.S. flag rise in victory over the stadium. Before the '68 event came to an end, she joined three other relay team members in another gold medal ceremony. When the last race had been run, she felt drained. "I had enjoyed my career and its rewards, but I had gotten to the point that I was really tired of running. I'd been running competitively for so many years and it had taken tremendous self-discipline to keep my body in condition. After the Olympics was over, I didn't even run across the street."

Wyomia, who earned her B.A. degree from Tennessee State, moved to California in late 1968 where she married Art Simburg, a representative for the German manufacturer of Puma track shoes. The Simburgs settled in Los Angeles in 1969 where Wyomia soon devoted her time to being a housewife and mother with the arrival of a daughter in the early '70s. When friends asked her if she'd go back to track, she said, jokingly, "I'd make a comeback if they paid you."

It didn't seem a likely happening in the late 1960s. But in the 1970s, the International Track Association was formed and one of its early invitations went to Wyomia. She agreed to try and started working out in early 1973 to get ready for the first meet of the new group at Pocatello, Idaho. She lost in that meet and didn't do any better in the second event on the tour. More than a few observers suggested a sprinter can't come back after a five-year layoff. Wyomia stuck with it and began to win some of her races. By the end of that first season, she had won eight of eighteen, enough to make her the leading money winner in women's events.

However, she wasn't too satisfied with her poor winning percentage. She set her sights on 1974 and started right off with a victory in the first meet. The year 1973 hadn't been a loss after all, as she said in '74. "It helped me this year. I was in better condition and my style improved. I always had a slow start and my reflexes were very slow after the five-year layoff. I was making too many moves at the beginning of the race. But as 1973 went by, I got things into proper order. My overall form was as good as it had been before, and once I got my start in good shape, things started to pick up."

As the 1974 season progressed, Wyomia blossomed into one of the top crowd pleasers. At both indoor and outdoor meets, she could be depended on to turn in times that compared well with the most publicized amateur women runners. Her 10.3 at El Paso, running into a 12-mile wind, was extraordinary. If the wind had been a more normal 4–5 mph, she might well have beaten the world record. Wyomia maintained her hot pace, remaining literally unbeatable. She won all twenty-two races on the tour and for the second time was leading money winner among women performers. It was generally agreed hers was one of a number of efforts that helped give pro track respectability with track fans.

For all that, Wyomia maintained her perspective on the meaning of sports in her life. She enjoyed running, but her family came first and she cautioned young aspirants to approach competition with a balanced outlook. "There's a lot of emphasis placed on winning and not enough on competing and just enjoying it. If you start out young and don't do well, you can suffer an ego loss. People should set goals for themselves that can be reached. You can't win all the time, but you might set a goal of getting out of the blocks better or improving on your last race time. I think it's really good for girls to participate in sports as long as they don't get hung up on winning all the time."

She also feels her success in pro track is her way of helping to promote women's role in the sport. "I've always felt that women's track and field in the United States has been on the bottom of the totem pole. People hardly realize women run other than every four years. I believe we should get just as much recognition as the men do. In Europe women are looked on as highly as men in this sport, if not more. In the United States this year, the men had their AAU championships at the University of California at Los Angeles where 20,000 people watched. The women's meet was held separately in Bakersfield where 5,000 is a large crowd. Properly, both men and women should take part in the same finals held in the same place."

8

MELISSA BELOTE
Swimming

The first World Women's Invitational Swim Meet, held at East Los Angeles College in February 1973, attracted a good share of press coverage. It was the first major swim meet of the year and the entrants, limited to finalists at the 1972 Olympic Games, included such well-known names as Australia's Shane Gould and Beverly Whitfield and the U.S.'s Deena Deardurff and Shirley Babashoff. Many reporters covering the event concentrated on these often publicized names and paid relatively little attention to a soft-spoken 132-pound, fair-skinned sixteen-year-old named Melissa Belote.

The story was familiar to her. It had happened in Munich in 1972 when she had reached a level of success attained by few in the grueling world of competitive swimming. There, too, the glare of the spotlight mostly focused on Shane Gould's efforts to approach Mark Spitz's all-winning assault on the men's world record book. Yet Melissa had what would otherwise have been hailed as a sensational Olympic series that equaled Shane's in gold medals won, and estab-

1. The awesomely skilled Babe Didrikson Zaharias sinks a putt on the way to one of her many golf titles.

2. Cathy Rigby demonstrates the "Rigby Scale," a gymnastic move she invented on the way to winning a silver medal at the 1970 World Games in Ljubljana, Yugoslavia.

3. Cathy Rigby works on the balance beam at Ljubljana, Yugoslavia during the 1970 World Games. By winning a silver medal in this category, Cathy became the first U.S. woman gymnast to do that well in a major international meet.

4. Billie Jean King, first woman tennis player to win over $100,000 in prize money in a year.

5. Robyn Smith left the world of high-fashion modeling to become one of the foremost jockeys in the United States.

6. Shirley "Cha Cha" Muldowney shows off some leisure wear (left) and 7. her drag-racing uniform complete with fireproof gloves and boots (right). 8. Below she runs through a spectacular burnout maneuver before taking her drag racing "Funny Car" to speeds of 200 mph and over on a quarter-mile strip.

9. Micki King displays the perfect body control that made her one of the all-time greats in diving.

10. Little Mary Decker, only fifteen years old, waits to compete against runners with years more experience.

11. Pigtails flying, Mary Decker held first place, as usual, on the way to a victory in the 880 at the 1974 Sunkist Invitational Track Meet at Los Angeles' Forum.

12. Theresa Shank poised for a jump shot against East Stroudsburg State College, February 2, 1974, at the Villanova University field house.

13. Wyomia Tyus takes a practice lap preparing for the 1974 pro track season.

14. After another victory in the 1974 pro tour, Wyomia Tyus talks it over with the track announcer.

15. Melissa Belote shows the power of her backstroke, one of the most demanding strokes in swimming, as she cuts through the water.

16. Ann Henning, speed-skating champion, takes a tight corner.

17. Barbara Ann Cochran, ski champion, gives a delighted winner's wave.

lished Melissa as an all-time great in her specialty, the backstroke.

At the World Women's Invitational, she went quietly about her tasks and won in everything she tried. In the 100-yard backstroke, she easily outdistanced a glittering field, beating her nearest rival, Canada's Donna Marie Gurr to the finish line by three seconds with a fine time of 58.9 seconds. She was even more impressive in the 200-yard backstroke, her time of 2:06.7 giving her a gaping margin over second-place finisher Deborah Palmer of Australia, who clocked 2:16.2. In addition, she teamed with Cathy Carr, Deena Deardurff and Shirley Babashoff, all former Olympic teammates, for a third win in the 400-medley relay. All in all, Melissa's first top-level competition since the Munich Games indicated she was still devoted to the arduous training needed to stay in world-class condition and that she might be one of the few U.S. women willing to stay with such a demanding schedule long enough for a try at a second Olympics, this time the 1976 event in Montreal, Canada.

As Melissa indicated, she didn't worry too much about lack of publicity. She had started swimming because she enjoyed it and the satisfaction of doing well was a fine reward in itself. Then, perhaps, there was the secret feeling of confusing the experts. For in her own steadfast way, she had come from obscurity to startle the swimming world in the first place by making the 1972 Olympic team and had compounded that by going on to be one of the mainstays at Munich. So even though the odds might be against her repeating at Montreal—only limited support was available to amateur swimmers generally, and women swimmers in particular, to continue training once past high school age—no one counted her out.

She had, after all, come a long way in one of the more difficult forms of swimming. The backstroke doesn't look as glamorous as the freestyle or the butterfly, facts that helped account for the smaller notice given to backstrokers than other swimming specialists. But it requires every bit as much skill as the others and probably a little more. A good backstroke artist must not only master a stroke that is inherently more awkward than other basic strokes, but must also overcome the psychological urge to know where one is going. The Australian crawl or the butterfly allows the swimmer to keep his or her eyes focused on the route ahead, but the backstroker must keep in an almost perfectly straight line while looking at the sky or the roof of the swimming pool.

Of course, for Melissa, it was the fact that she could do this that made her concentrate on the backstroke. "The pool I trained in had a very large amount of chlorine and it was terrible on the eyes. I figured that if I swam on my back I wouldn't have to worry about the chlorine. It worked out well."

Melissa started swimming at the tender age of ten in her hometown of Springfield, Virginia, in 1966. At first, it was just for fun, but it soon became apparent that she was good at it. She could outrace her friends from one side of a pool to the other and her style seemed to improve each time she went into the water. She started taking swimming lessons in a local pool and impressed her instructors with her ability. Before she was in her teens, Melissa had developed into the best backstroke swimmer in her area. By the time she entered Lee High School in Springfield, she was already being groomed for top-level competition by swimming coach Ed Solotar. Melissa took up the strenuous requirements for swimming success without complaint. Like thousands of other hopefuls the world over, she accepted a schedule that called for hours of swimming every day, usually involving several in the early morning before the school day started and still more after her classmates were home relaxing with friends or sprawled in front of the TV set. To build up the great endurance needed for championship swimming called for going back and forth across the pool hundreds of times every day, a task many times harder than that faced by a runner. Water is over sixty times denser than air, which accounts for the longer time a swimmer requires to cover the same distance a champion runner can cover.

The demands of swimming go far beyond that needed for most sports. Though the hours of training might be the same, the great exertion needed to overcome water resistance is far more tiring than almost any other sport. Champion pole vaulter Bob Seagren found this out while taking swimming lessons in preparation for taking part in the ABC-TV 1974 Superstars competition. After following the directions of a swim coach for several weeks he said wearily, "These lessons are killing me." The experience made him state that swimmers are the world's fittest athletes and certainly among the most dedicated.

As the 1970s began, Melissa probably would have agreed as she intensified her workouts in response to coach Solotar's urgings. Though she had countless hours of practice behind her, her muscles still ached after some days of rigorous activity. To help her forget this and perhaps relieve some of the tension, she developed the habit of shouting as she made her way up and down the pool, legs pumping steadily in a rhythmic kick, arms reaching up and back. "It's my secret weapon," she said. "I'm yelling at myself. It helps me concentrate. When I don't yell, I don't do well."

For the most part, though, Melissa did well indeed. In meet after meet on the East Coast she added to a growing cache of medals and trophies in her Virginia home. As 1970 and '71 went by, she traveled to meets in other parts of the country where she gained experience against top-level swimmers. She didn't always win, but she usually was in the top three or four finishers in her events. Despite this, she was not given much attention on the national backstroke scene. Most of the star swimmers for years had come from California, particularly from the Arden Hills Swim Club and George Haines's Santa Clara Swim Club whose alumni included most U.S. medal winners in the Olympics of the '60s. Melissa, on the other hand, was from the East and had not even competed much in the West.

However, her times were good and she wasn't completely ignored. By 1971, most experts ranked her among the top U.S. women backstrokers. In 1971, she was considered to be the fourth best in her category in the country. But fourth best wasn't good enough for a swimmer to win the coveted berth on the Olympic team. Even Melissa had some secret doubts about her chances, though her coach insisted she could hold her own with the best.

Both Solotar and Melissa knew she would have the chance to prove herself in the summer of 1971. One of the most important meets of the year was scheduled at the Santa Clara pool and Melissa would get the chance to try her skills against all the fastest backstrokers including the U.S. champion, Susie Atwood. Aiming for this, Melissa put in every spare moment to polish her style. To the coach's commands she began her first laps in the early dawn hours and was at it again in the evening. She did very well in the meets that preceded the Santa Clara event, but the question remained whether the fourteen-year-old could come through when the attention of all the top swimming experts in the country was on her.

The months went by and finally the time came to fly to the San Francisco Bay Area. For Melissa it was a nervous but exciting time. She had a tough challenge ahead, but she was in the company of such great names as Susie Atwood, Shirley Babashoff, Mark Spitz and the others expected to spearhead the American Olympic efforts the next year.

Somehow the days went by as Melissa continued her daily swim routine and tried to banish worry from her mind. Almost in a daze, she found herself in the finals of the 200 meter with Susie Atwood and other highly ranked swimmers on the starting blocks around her. The order "get ready" came and the swimmers got into position, their backs to the water. Seconds later the starting gun went off and eight slender bodies were churning the water on the first 50 meters. Shouting to herself, Melissa picked up her pace, moving steadily along in unison with several others including Susie Atwood. The pace was a hot one, but Melissa kept up with it and at the halfway mark was up with the leaders. By the 150-meter mark, she had a slight lead and to the rising torrent of screams from the crowd, she maintained it to touch the tile at the end line first.

The upset made the experts realize Melissa would be someone to watch when the Olympic trials took place the following summer. For Melissa, it was a vital turning point. "I knew then that I was as good as anyone in the world. Confidence is very important in swimming."

This surge of confidence showed in her achievements after that. Her times slowly got better and she splashed to victory time after time. When she went to Chicago for the Olympic trials in August 1972, no one discounted her chances of making the team. But Melissa knew she couldn't let down. The girls she'd edged out at Santa Clara were every bit as eager to turn the tables, and there was always the danger some young unknown would catch fire as Melissa had the year before. But she was in excellent condition, and though only fifteen, a relative veteran. Showing tremendous power, she entered the finals in both the 100 and 200 meter and streaked to the finish each time a good few yards ahead of her nearest opponent.

Two months later she was aboard an airliner headed for West Germany. Before long she was eagerly taking part in the pageantry of the world's greatest amateur sports event, marching behind the American flag bearer in the opening ceremonies at the huge new stadium built for the Olympics and exchanging souvenirs with athletes from all over the globe in the Olympic village. But there wasn't too much time for socializing.

As soon as the team was settled, they had to sharpen their reflexes with the usual intensive drills. Melissa and the others had to still the butterflies that arose when they considered the caliber of swimmers to be faced and the fact that as many as a billion people might watch them on TV. The center of attention, though, wasn't the backstrokers or even the U.S. women freestylers, but the amazing exploits of Mark Spitz and Australia's superstar, Shane Gould.

The first order of business was to do well in the qualifying heats. It wasn't necessary to win these heats, but Melissa had to place in the top three in each race to move on to the gold medal arena. The large crowds jamming the sparkling new Schwimmhalle, far beyond anything Melissa had seen before, and the staring unhuman eyes of countless TV cameras might have shaken the cool of an athlete with a dozen years experience, much less a teen-ager. But Melissa showed little fear as she went about her business. With strong, decisive strokes she accomplished her objective, qualifying in the 100-meter and 200-meter backstroke and swimming the backstroke leg of the U.S. 400-meter medley relay team.

But the true test lay just ahead. The night before her first final, the 200-meter backstroke, Melissa found it wasn't easy to fall asleep. It was a thrill to have come this far, only a handful of girls in the world ever get the chance to swim in an Olympic competition. But it would still be tough to go back home a loser. Of course, five of eight girls the next day would fail to get a medal, and with the world's best taking part the slightest mistake—a poor start, a leg cramp, a slow turn—and the medal would fade away.

Despite misgivings shared by all the entrants, the mid-October day arrived. The program moved along and the officials called for the 200-meter backstroke finalists. Moments later, eight sturdy-looking girls marched in single file across the bright yellow tiles of the Schwimmhalle as the crowd applauded. The field included two other U.S. girls besides Melissa and a strong entry from the rapidly improving East German women's team. The girls shook their arms to relax their muscles, some took a brief dip in the practice area behind the starting blocks. Then the loudspeaker boomed out the starting call. The girls moved onto the small platforms at one end of the 50-meter-long pool, the overhead lights reflecting rippling circles in the bright turquoise water.

Melissa well knew she approached a possible high point in her career. Of course, if she lost the race, she still had two more chances for a medal, but it would take so much pressure off to get off on the right foot . . . The officials gave the ready signal and the girls faced away from the water and the long black lines on the pool floor that marked off the lanes. The crowd fell silent as the second warning sounded. Thousands of bodies slid forward on their seats as the girls' expressions indicated the great effort to hear the "go" signal the split second it was given. The official raised his blank pistol, pulled the trigger and the whole area sprang to life.

The eight bodies hit the water almost as one and soon were away, arms flashing briefly in the air before disappearing into the ruffled water.

Melissa's voice was drowned out by the thunder of the crowd, but she continued to egg herself on. Her strokes were smooth and effective. When she made the first turn, half the group already had slipped behind a little. When the 100-meter mark arrived, Melissa was slightly ahead and the split showed she was ahead of the world's record. At the three-quarters, Melissa was several lengths ahead of two others, but they still could catch her. As she came off the final turn, Melissa strained to increase her speed just a little, her body responding like a finely tuned instrument. The Americans in the audience, her coach and team members jumped and yelled encouragement, though all she could hear was the dull rippling noise of the surrounding water. Now she sensed her quest was almost over. Her fingers stretched back on each pass, searching for the cool solid surface at the finish. Then she touched and the electronic plate installed in the pool wall closed a circuit to the timing clock. As she pulled off her cap and swam a few strokes to drain the tension, she knew she had her first gold medal. Seconds later the crowd roared as the flashing numbers on the huge scoreboard at one end of the hall gave evidence that Virginia's pride had set a new world record.

Soon after, Melissa stood proudly on the winner's stand as an official placed the cord holding the gleaming golden circle with the five linked rings on one side (symbolizing the five continents joined together in sport) around her neck. Then, drops of water glistening on her close-cropped blond hair, she came to attention as "The Star-Spangled Banner" played and the flag of the United States moved slowly to the top of the hall, flanked below by the two runner-up banners.

It was a thrill Melissa was to feel twice more before she left Munich. Her second gold medal was shared with three team members for a first place in the 400-meter medley relay in which Melissa's backstroke leg led off and gave the quartet an initial lead it never relinquished. Finally came a third gold medal in the 100-meter backstroke, in which Melissa set a second world record, marking her as the world's greatest in that class.

Her return home was not the Hollywood-style one of Mark Spitz, but if she got little national attention, she was acclaimed by the home folks. Her homecoming to Springfield, Virginia, was the occasion of a great celebration including a parade in her honor. And, in early 1973, she broke tradition when she won the Arch McDonald Award of the Washington, D.C., Touchdown Club, marked normally for "the area boy who makes good," usually in football. The judges could think of no one, boy or girl, who more deserved the honor. At the awards banquet, Melissa graciously accepted a standing ovation from the audience which included many famous names in sports and many important government officials.

It did not make her name a household word, but that didn't bother her. "I never worried about not getting much publicity. Swimming has been wonderful to me. I have met a great bunch of girls, gotten to travel and I am very proud that I was the first girl invited by the Washington Touchdown Club to receive an award."

9

SHIRLEY MULDOWNEY

Drag Racing

Learning that a girl has the nickname of "Cha Cha," it's easy to imagine her being a Hollywood starlet or a svelte member of a Las Vegas chorus line. And, in truth, long-legged, well-proportioned Shirley Muldowney looks the part. But her major avocation is about as far removed from that of sterile beauty as possible. Cha Cha Muldowney is ranked as one of the best there is in the dangerous, death-defying sport of drag racing. In a field that seems to symbolize rugged, "he man" heroics, petite Shirley fought her way to the top by meeting the best male drivers in the sport head-on and often beating them at their own game.

As a youngster growing up in Mt. Clemens, Michigan, there wasn't too much indication of the turn her career would take. Though she was more agile and coordinated than the average girl, Shirley didn't seem to take any greater interest in sports than her peer group. She liked dancing, dating and wearing pretty clothes. Of course, if her school was involved in an important football or basketball game, she would often scream with the loudest in urging them on to victory.

Nor was she overly intrigued with the number one product of her home state, the automobile. In fact, she couldn't even drive a car when she got married in her late teens toward the end of the 1950s. Her husband, however, had a long-time love affair with high-performance cars. He had been taking cars apart and putting them back together again from his early high school years, and he had already been in many a drag race by the time he won Shirley for his bride. Soon after the wedding, he taught Shirley to drive. Once she got behind the wheel of a car, Shirley quickly succumbed to her husband's enthusiasm for four-wheeled vehicles.

She began by watching local drag races, sometimes when her husband took part, sometimes joining him as a spectator when they got the chance to go to big-time meets. It didn't take long for her to learn the rules. Drag racing almost always took the form of an elimination with two drivers at a time vying with each other to see who could cover a course measuring a quarter of a mile—1,320 feet—in the shortest time. The one who did this then went up against the winner of another dual match-up and the process continued until two finalists thundered down the asphalt lanes to battle for first place.

As Shirley observed from watching her husband and his co-workers, it looked simple, but the race itself was only the tip of an iceberg. Grooming a car for drag racing took many long hours during the week and immediately preceding the race. The team had to check the car out and adjust many mechanical parts from the suspension system to the engine valves, cams and rods. Then everyone had to work out the proper strategy to meet the particular conditions of the track on which they would run and to counter the abilities of the competition.

The driver had to work with the crew on all these things and also get as much time behind the wheel as possible to build up experience in the demanding technique of split-second reaction. In a sport where the slightest loss of control could cause the vehicle to flip in the air end-over-end or smash into a metal guard rail at speeds of 100 mph and better, where the fuel mixture usually was far more volatile and explosive than the propellants in the family car, coolness under pressure was vital. Cha Cha knew full well that a first-rate drag racer had to practice the requirements of high-speed driving to the point that the way the wheel was turned or the brakes were applied would be done unthinkingly, automatically, the moment instinct alerted the driver to danger. And she knew too it wouldn't be the easiest thing to achieve this experience where the typical run for an average driver took 15 seconds or less and, for a successful professional, from 10 to 11 seconds on down to 7, 8, or 9 seconds.

Still, the excitement of flashing down the short, black-top strip at breakneck speed appealed to her. She was aware of the dangers, but she couldn't abide standing on the sidelines. She asked her husband to let her race and he obliged by supplying her with a 1940 Ford powered by a hulking Cadillac V-8 engine. With this, she started entering local drag races in the regular stock car category. She didn't win very often, but she held her own, getting into the group of sixteen or thirty-two entries who qualified for the finals on occasion and gradually polishing her driving technique. In the early 1960s, she moved up to a more powerful Corvette, next a 348 tri-power Chevrolet and then a 1963 Super Stock Plymouth.

She drove all of these cars far faster over a quarter mile than any housewife would take the family car on the freeway, but still she could hit only a little over 100 mph, even in the '63 Plymouth. Meanwhile, dragster drivers who piloted long, low-slung vehicles that looked like Erector Set creations, with big engines stuck in the middle or on the rear end, were regularly reaching speeds of 170–180 miles an hour from a standing start and covering the quarter mile in less than 10 seconds. Of course, the faster the speed, the greater the risk of steel-rending mishaps or shuddering engine blowups, but none of this fazed Shirley.

It was the challenge that counted. Like her male counterparts, she wanted to be where the action was wildest and the demands on driver ability the greatest.

The Plymouth began to seem too tame and she asked her husband to get her a dragster. As she told a reporter, "The Plymouth was an automatic. I got tired of pushing the buttons. That's not my idea of a race car. I told my husband I wanted a dragster." He complied with her request by building her one powered by a small-block Chevrolet engine. Before long she was blazing down tracks across the United States at speeds of 170 and 180 mph.

At the same time, she was fighting another battle, this time one of words with the sanctioning authorities. The officials of the National Hot Rod Association, American Hot Rod Association and other groups that supervised the major drag-racing events were reluctant about granting professional credentials to a member of the "weaker sex." There were arguments that it might be bad for the sport if a woman were to be seriously injured in a nationally publicized event. Others felt that drag racing was a man's sport and should stay that way. They noted that there was no bar against women racing in local, unsanctioned meets or in amateur classes; that should be enough.

However, Shirley and such women drivers as Judi Boertman, Paula Murphy and Della Woods persisted. If they were willing to brave the dangers of racing, why should they be penalized just because of sex, they argued. Besides, they felt that if they could prove they could achieve performances as good as male drivers, they should have the opportunity to compete.

It wasn't an overnight thing, but the persistent requests of the women finally paid off. By the mid-1960s, they had the right to try for racing approval the same way as any other driver. Cha Cha, already a skilled racer with dozens of races to her credit, easily won her professional credentials.

And she continued to win the male drivers over to her side with excellent performances and her demonstration of cool concentration in desperate situations. One incident that impressed the driving fraternity occurred at Orange County International Raceway in 1967. Cradled in the steel protective cage at the rear of her

Chevy-engined dragster, Cha Cha shot from the starting line in an eliminator race and accelerated down the strip at blinding speed. It was a good run and she flashed into the speed-measuring section around the finish line at over 180 mph. She hit the drag chute release to start slowing the car down and quickly realized by the absence of a sudden pull that it wasn't working. She tried her brakes and they, too, wouldn't respond.

There was nothing to do but ride it out. As she sat helplessly in the ground-hugging long-railed machine, it went on to the end of the track and past, bumping over a short stretch of sand and grass, and headed right for a chain link fence. With a screeching, jarring sensation, it sliced through the fence into a stand of woods on the other side. The vehicle had been slowed by the impact, but still had enough momentum to plow through several hundred feet of brush and trees, finally coming to rest in a crumpled, smoking heap. But the safety gear had done its job. When Shirley's husband and the crew reached her, they found she was ready with a grim smile and a wisecrack or two. She was shaken up, but otherwise unhurt. The home-built dragster was a total loss, but within a few days' time Cha Cha was making plans for a new vehicle.

Hair-raising crashes are considered a normal part of drag racing, and Cha Cha had her share in the next few years. The most feared mishaps are those involving fire. In one race, the car skidded on a wet track and, as Shirley fought to get the vehicle back in position, the stress on the engine became too great and it blew a rod. Seconds later, the highly volatile fuel mixture leaked onto hot metal and burst into flame. Bright orange streaks flickered around Cha Cha's fire-suited figure as she fought to control the car. The heat became so intense the brake fluid boiled and the parachute went up in smoke. Once more Cha Cha found herself careening down the track with no way to stop. However, she wasn't going too fast and the vehicle came to rest before going past the end line. Again Cha Cha walked away without a scratch.

With this kind of courage, Cha Cha won over all the doubters among the racing fraternity. "The men always said, 'Just wait until she has a fire.' I had one and I did all I was supposed to, so now they seem to think I'm okay."

Soon after her Orange County accident, Cha Cha was again on the trail of drag-racing prize money. She still liked dragsters, but began to consider trying her hand at a new breed of drag vehicles, funny cars. Funny cars had been evolving in the early 1960s into one of the most colorful, crowd-pleasing class of drag racers. The impetus for them was the development by auto companies of new, very powerful engines that promised horsepower outputs of up to 1,500, hundreds more than in conventional dragsters or stock cars. These engines were installed at first in modified production cars. The changes in the early days involved moving the position of the wheels forward of their normal location to provide the right weight balance for the souped-up engine. This gave the cars an ugly duckling appearance that caused one track announcer to say, "look at those funny cars coming up to the line!" The name stuck even though later designs were as streamlined and good-looking a group of vehicles as could be found in the sport.

By the late 1960s, the funny car had changed drastically. Instead of using stock-bodied cars, builders had gone to making what amounted to cut-down dragster chassis covered with plastic body shells. The body shells, according to the rules set up by the NHRA, AHRA, et al., had to closely imitate a regular late-model production car. The shells themselves were carefully crafted out of fiberglass by skilled experts and then were painted in a rainbow of colors with intricate designs and eye-catching color schemes.

The combination of high speeds and external forms that onlookers could associate with cars they drove themselves or saw around them on the highway, quickly made funny cars highly popular. In a few years' time, they became one of the three or four professional categories, a must at any drag meet and one of the classes that attracted the best drivers. In the early 1970s, the names entered in the prestige national meets in this category read like a Who's Who in drag racing—people like Don "The Snake" Prudhomme, national champion of top fuel dragsters for much of the '60s, his arch-rival, Tom "Mongoose" McEwen, Texas whirlwind Gene Snow, the Midwest champion Don Schumacher, dragster great Jerry Ruth and many others.

Shirley and her husband looked around for a way to get into this booming area and finally got the chance to buy a used car from Detroit driver Connie Kalitta. With the nickname "Bounty Huntress" emblazoned in gold script letters on the sides of a bright yellow Plymouth sedan body striped with bright red bars on the hood and roof, Shirley became a familiar figure at leading funny car meets. As the '70s started, she was regularly turning speeds of over 200 mph and covering the short drag course in 7 and 8 seconds.

In 1971, she really came into her own. Racing against the most successful funny car drivers, she won her share against the best of them. In the summer she entered the International Hot Rod Association's Summernationals. Almost effortlessly, she streaked down the course at well over 200 mph and qualified for the handful of drivers that made up the actual eliminator field. In the finals, she posed a strong challenge to the otherwise all-male roster, reaching the last pairings before bowing out.

A little later, in September, she vied for top honors in the even more prestigious National Hot Rod Association Nationals meet, held every year at the famed Indianapolis Speedway in Indianapolis, Indiana. The great names of funny car racing were all there—Prudhomme, Snow, McEwen, Schumacher, Ed "The Ace" McCulloch, Jim "Fireman" Dunn. There were dozens of others fighting to make a good enough time in the qualifying heats to become one of the sixteen drivers in the finals. Many of the top experts fell by the wayside early. Prudhomme's team couldn't get the car running smoothly and he never "got off the trailer," and McEwen wasn't able to accelerate his Hot Wheels Plymouth Duster to a good enough elapsed time.

The crowd edged forward on its seats when Shirley's gleaming Mustang came to the staging area. The crew made final preparation as Shirley buckled her safety harness. Her long brunette hair and womanly form were hidden in the head-to-toe aluminized fire suit that resembled the astronaut's garb from which it evolved. A fire resistant hood, pierced only by two small eyeholes that housed special quartz goggles, covered her features, giving her a science-fictionlike appearance.

The official gave her the OK after the fiberglass flip-top body was lowered into place and latched down to the chassis. First came the burnout. The car's tires were coated by mechanics with a special gooey-looking compound. Then the car lurched forward a few hundred feet, sending billowing clouds of blue-gray smoke in all directions. This maneuver is used to warm the tires and to lay down tracks of rubber compound to give a good bite between tires and roadway so the wheels don't spin and lose precious forward energy. Under careful direction of her crew, Cha Cha backed the car into starting position keeping the tires in the tracks just laid down.

Moments later, the starter pushed the electric button to turn on the warning light on the Christmas Tree pole. As soon as the light glowed yellow, Cha Cha hit the gas pedal and thundered past the now green "go" light onto the mile-long runway. The car skittered a bit at the beginning as the air pressure on the smooth body surfaces created a lifting force trying to carry the car into the air. Then it straightened out to roar into the heart of the course with blurring intensity. It looked like a good run and thousands of voices screamed encouragement. In the blinking of an eye, the Mustang was at mid-course and seconds later was streaking past the lights of the finish line. Cha Cha hit the chute button and the gossamer, X-shaped parachute was soon floating behind, bringing the car to a speed low enough for the regular brakes to take hold.

As the crew rushed up, Cha Cha could see the glow of happiness in everyone's eyes. It seemed like a perfect effort. Moments later the public address system boomed out the news. She had covered the distance in 6.76 seconds (reaching a top speed of 215.31) and was assured of making it into the finals. With that achievement, Shirley arrived as one of drag-racing's elite. Gaining a quarter-mile time of under 7 seconds in one of the most important drag meets of the year was something only the very best drivers could claim. As it turned out, the next goal, winning the championship, eluded Cha Cha, for her car broke down in the first round. The winner turned out to be Ed McCulloch with a series of runs in the 6.6.-second area, but Cha Cha's efforts won her as much notice from fans and drag-racing experts as McCulloch's win.

In the years that have followed, Cha Cha has ranked as one of the foremost drivers in her sport. During 1972 and '73, she was generally considered one of the "top 5" in funny cars, along with Prudhomme, McEwen, Schumacher and Gene Snow. In the mid-1970s she switched her attention from funny cars to become a major contender in top fuel dragsters.

For all that, she enjoys being a woman. A homemaker, she has attended to the needs of her young son, proudly watching his progress through grade and high school and doing the things a mother usually does, including attending PTA meetings and little league games.

As she told *Hot Rod* magazine, "I like being the weaker sex. But I do think it's about time that women were treated equal. When I started racing, people discriminated against me because I was a woman. I like having doors opened for me. I also feel that some of the Lib people go to extremes. I want to be able to go to the track and look like a lady, but still be able to do a job like a man when I'm racing and get paid the same amount of money."

10

BARBARA ANN COCHRAN
Skiing

One sport in which women have long played a very active role is skiing. This isn't surprising, since in the places where skiing began, Scandinavia and Russia, for a long time skis and snowshoes were just about the only ways to get around in the wintertime in some regions. Thus, boys and girls learned to ski in remote areas almost as soon as they learned to walk. As races between men became formalized in the 1800s, women followed right along with competitions of their own.

Though skiing came to the New World along with many other European activities, it never gained quite the intense interest it attained in the old country. For one thing, many parts of the United States stayed relatively snow free all year round. For another, by the time large groups of people had settled such places as the Midwest and the Northeast, transportation methods had improved to the point that people could get from place to place in most instances without the aid of long narrow staves strapped to their feet. These conditions, plus the long tradition of winter sports overseas, resulted in American teams playing second fiddle, for the most part, to teams from abroad.

The years after World War II, though, brought an upsurge of interest in skiing in the United States. People were making more money and had more time to spend on leisure-time activities. And as sports reporters and TV brought stories of international ski meets, young people were increasingly attracted to the thrills of gliding down steep snow-clad mountainsides both for the fun of doing it and the challenge of outclassing other rivals.

A hotbed of these developments was New England, where the annals of skiing went back a good many years more than in other parts of the nation. In New England, as in Europe, skiing remained a family pastime. It was not uncommon on a winter's day to see mother, father, kids old and young, and assorted relations out playing follow-the-leader over winding white trails or learning the fine points of stopping, turning or climbing from one another.

From this environment, a few world-class skiers surfaced to give the United States a boost in international competition. In the early 1950s, Vermont's Andrea Mead Lawrence demonstrated awesome skills in all phases of the sport and won or placed high in both downhill racing and the tricky twists and turns of slalom racing against the world's best. She capped her career by winning two gold medals in the 1952 Olympics. After she retired, though, no U.S. skier came close to her feats for the rest of the 1950s or in the '60s. The general level of ability of American girls did rise during those years, but women skiers everywhere improved, and government support elsewhere insured them far more time to practice than most U.S. girls could afford.

For one New Englander, though, the lack of good practice facilities wasn't going to stand in the way. Gordon "Mickey" Cochran loved to ski and, after he settled his growing family in a small farmhouse on the shores of the Winooski River near Richmond, Vermont, he set about clearing room for a small ski slope on the hillside behind the house. He had seen to it that all his four children from Lindy, the youngest (six in 1960) to Marilyn, the oldest of his three daughters, started on skis early in life. As he watched them master each skiing technique, he felt sure all of them could be experts, given the proper supervision and training schedule.

One of his first moves in the early 1960s was to spend part of one summer constructing a homemade tow to the top of a nearby hill. With this in operation, he and the children could get more skiing in by being pulled up mechanically the 400 feet to the starting point rather than painfully climbing back with the herringbone technique. When the snows came, the shrieks, giggles and happy shouts of the Cochrans rang out over the countryside from early afternoon on school days until the last rays of the early setting sun disappeared from view.

Mickey Cochran enjoyed what he saw. His children all seemed to have natural athletic talent. They proved it when the family went to Mount Ascutney where many residents from the area congregated for winter activities. One popular event for the younger skiers was the "lollipop" race. All the small fry were invited to take part and a lollipop was given to everyone who crossed the finish line. The Cochran clan not only got a lollipop almost every time out, they generally led the pack across the line.

As Marilyn, Barbara Ann and the others neared their teens, they held their own against the toughest competition in the neighborhood. In fun races, the girls often edged out challenges from boys and rarely lost to other girls in regular events or in impromptu sweeps down local slopes. All of this inspired their father to help them bring their skills to razor-sharp precision. He helped set up body-building exercises and activities to sharpen their reflexes for all seasons of the year. To give them more time to practice, he set up lights along the 400-foot trail behind the house. As the children grew into young adulthood, he added a more demanding course, building a 1,200-foot rope tow for it on the slopes behind the farmhouse.

By the end of the '60s, the older Cochran children began demonstrating the fine pitch of skiing excellence their father's tutelage had provided. They entered a number of major events in New England and elsewhere and always gave a good showing. Many ski experts watched them in action and predicted they might well carry the major share of U.S. hopes in world competition. With three girls only a few years apart in age, the Cochrans could almost field an Olympic women's team of their own.

Stories circulated far and wide about the rigorous program Mickey Cochran set up to train his offspring, stories that might be a little exaggerated. For example, *Skiing* magazine reported an incident the mother of a girl friend of the Cochran girls said took place when her daughter went to Vermont one summer. "She went to Richmond to spend a few days with them—a little vacation, she thought. She came home early. 'My God, Mother,' she told me, 'that place is a training camp. We were up at six to cycle for twenty miles, then play tennis, then run some more miles, then lift weights all afternoon. That's what they do for fun—lift weights. I had to come home to get some rest.'"

While the Cochrans agreed they went through as many exercises as any athlete does to stay in condition, it really wasn't that extreme a case. Their normal preparations weren't dawn to dusk affairs, they told reporters and, while they might begin activities early, they got up at a normal hour and ate a regular breakfast before starting.

Whatever the exact facts, the pattern certainly worked. In the late '60s and in the early '70s, Marilyn and Barbara Ann regularly took part in the international ski tour and won their share of medals at such ski centers as Lake Placid, New York; Aspen, Colorado; and the great centers of snow sports in Switzerland, the French Alps, Austria, Germany and Italy. Their specialty was the slalom and giant slalom, challenging races in which the skier must go down a steep slope dotted with pairs of slender poles arranged to form a long series of "gates." The skier must whisk through these narrow openings at as fast a speed as possible without losing her balance or missing the entry. Often the contestant must contend with rutted snow, sudden bumps and the onslaught of fog or falling snow that obscures the course ahead. For success, perfect co-ordination of leg motion and the poles the skier uses for balance is needed, plus intense concentration on the dozens of sudden changes of direction. A slight distraction, the placement of one ski a little too far in the wrong direction and the racer can fall, possibly to twist or break an ankle, or miss one of the gates which means instant disqualification for that run.

The coaching of father Cochran had been stern but effective. Marilyn and Barbara Ann treated the most rugged course in Europe as though it were the hill behind their Vermont home. Europeans marveled at the speed the girls could maintain while darting in and out of the toothpicklike rows of stakes. As the 1972 Olympic Games neared, both Marilyn and Barbara Ann were ranked among the top ten women's slalom artists and were given chances—though outside ones, considering the strength of the European women—for medals at Sapporo.

Through the summer and fall of 1971, all the Cochrans redoubled their conditioning efforts. They ran for miles each day, added pounds to their weight-lifting program and performed exercises prescribed by the U. S. Olympic ski coach Hank Tauber. As usual, when the snow was on the slopes again and the pre-Olympic trials got underway, the Cochrans were in excellent physical condition and all but Lindy made the U.S. team. (Lindy did well enough to qualify as an alternate, however.)

As diminutive Marilyn and Barbara Ann, both only a

little over five feet tall, continued to perform brilliantly at Alpine-style meets in late 1971, U.S. hopes rose. However, everyone was aiming for the Olympics and all the nations of Europe had young, very talented representatives. Austria had blazingly fast eighteen-year-old Annemarie Proell, who won the World Cup in 1971 and was considered good enough to win all three Alpine events—women's downhill, the slalom and the giant slalom. And France had one of its most talented teams ever with such great skiers as Françoise Macchi, Michèle Jacot, Isabelle Mir, Florence Steurer, Britt Lafforgue, and a promising newcomer, Danièle Debernard. There also were athletes on almost every other team with the potential to win the gold medal.

If all of this bothered the Cochrans, it didn't show as they made their way around the ski world before the time for going to Japan was at hand. They were cordial and affable, seeming to enjoy joking and idle chatter with their friends when they weren't out on the ski runs. They felt confident they could hold their own with any skier in the world and, with luck, could prove it in Japan.

By the end of January 1972 the Cochran family had shifted its base of operations to Sapporo. The setting for the Alpine events proved to be magnificent, with the slalom courses nestled high on volcanic Mount Teine, called the Roof of Sapporo, which jutted high into the winter air above the industrial town. Nearby rose another snow-clad mountain, Eniwa, down whose slopes the downhill racers could sweep past a vista that included the sparkling surface of Lake Shikotsu. The courses were difficult, as befits the most glamorous skiing event of all, with the slalom gates spaced out in exacting patterns on a hazardous slope of Mount Teine.

The problems posed by the course were seen all too well by all Alpine hopefuls as they took their practice runs and got the feel of the terrain. The ground was scooped into unpredictable hollows that changed subtly as the forces of wind and occasional snowfalls varied the form and properties of the snow surface. The high mountain reaches were subject to sudden weather changes that included rolling fogs that blinded the racers as they twisted and turned through the closely placed, flag-topped gates. Heavy favorite Annemarie Proell shook her head after trying the slalom layouts. "I feel confident about the downhill, but I don't think I'll sweep all three medals. The slalom is very steep at the top and not to my liking."

When the skiing competition got underway, Annemarie's predictions proved accurate. She won the downhill, but fared poorly in the slaloms. The American women were shut out in the downhill as expected and the treacherous nature of the slaloms and the great strength of the French team made most onlookers give the United States little chance for a medal in either slalom or giant slalom. If anyone could do it, all agreed, it would be the Cochran girls, but Marilyn had her problems and the pressure fell on the shoulders of Barbara Ann.

In the draw for the first of two runs in the slalom finals, Barbara got a relatively late starting position as did most of the top skiers. It was a possible stumbling block for the initial run because the course could be in bad shape from the assault of the first groups of contestants. For the second run, though, this was compensated for by reversing the starting order with the last skier in the first run becoming number one on the second run, and so on. In Barbara's case, it meant a number fifteen start the second time, which could be an advantage if the low-hanging, dark gray clouds deposited a new layer of snow between races. Were that to happen, the early skiers would pack it down and make it faster for those who followed them.

But Barbara knew the first order of business was to do well in her first try. With the slower skiers going ahead that time, the clockings that appeared on the electronic scoreboard at the foot of the course were relatively slow. The course became progressively slower as each skier slashed down the slope, packing down the snow but also cutting into it and scarring it in places where some missed a turn and fell headlong to one side or hooked a ski on a gate and sent white slivers spraying in all directions.

But Barbara thought positively and blanked all the dangers of falling from her mind as she took the starting signal and pushed off down the slopes. She built up a good initial speed and carried through with tight, accurate turns as she made her way downhill, oblivious of the lines of spectators along the pine-clad sides who shouted unheard encouragement in the whistling wind. The running numbers on TV screens marked her progress and showed a surprisingly good story. When she came out of the last gates and sped beneath the large white canvas sign that marked the endline, the figures froze in a welcome pattern. She had bettered all other times by a number of seconds, an achievement that promised to give her a major advantage with an earlier start on the second run.

But Barbara was aware that some of the best skiers were yet to come. One by one they streaked down the course, each demonstrating catlike quickness and cool daring as they cut unbelievably close to the poles on each turn and fought for hundredths of a second advantage at each gate. When all had finished run number one, though, the scoreboard showed Barbara still ahead. But three top-ranked girls were close, within a second of her time, and all would get the chance to ski ahead of her in the second round. It was certain one or more would post two-run totals that would call for Barbara's very best effort to win the medal.

As the skiers side-stepped back up the mountain for the last run, they anxiously studied the weather and stared at the gates to see if anything had changed from the first time. Maintenance crews were replacing poles and smoothing over rough spots, but the wind was rising and showers of snowflakes were streaking down. More ominously, the clouds were pressing down closer to the land and, at the top, wet, clinging fog alternatively was covering and uncovering the stretches of the course.

There was a certain nervous tension in the air as the first women got the call to get round two underway. If the weather closed in too much, the race might be called off and all might have the agonizing overnight wait for another attempt. It was something few desired because it could completely throw off the hard-won psychology of race day. But the weather capriciously lightened each time it looked as though things might be too severe to continue. The runs began and the French girls demonstrated their great ability as Danièle Debernard and Florence Steurer took top spots momentarily with spine-tingling runs. Britt Lafforgue took off from the top with grim determination and she shaved each turn as close as seemed possible, moving down the string of gates faster than anyone had gone before. The experts watching her on TV commented that it was a pace no one was likely to match but then, just as the gold medal was well within her grasp, she made a slight mistake, she changed balance ever so slightly on a turn and couldn't recover in time, her hopes going up in white sprays of snow as she tumbled to the ground.

Still, Barbara had to come up with as good a run as she'd ever made to overtake the other French girls. She kept telling herself she could only try her hardest. As she told a reporter afterward, "I kept saying, 'even if I fall I had that good first run to remember.'"

Then her number was called and she was at the starting gate, hunched forward, skis even and parallel, her white ski shirt with the red stripes on the shoulders and the blue bands on the arms marked with white stars blending in with the swirling snow. The "go" sign came and she jabbed her ski poles into the snow to start into the fog-shrouded course, picking up speed as she headed for the first gate. The turn was well executed, she hit the snow with a quick, pistonlike jab with her downhill pole to trigger the turn, stood up slightly to take weight off the skis as she skidded inward toward the red poles that formed the gate. In the blink of an eye she was through, shifting her weight and setting the edges of the skis for the next turn.

Down she went, poles flashing, skis shifting just the right amount, body working ceaselessly in response to the reflexes gained through long years of training to keep everything rhythmically synchronized. She cut the turns as close as possible without making them so sharp that a ski would get too far out of line or a pole would not be ready for the right darting movement. Through her close-fitting goggles she strained to see the next target, her mind having to work to tolerances of hundredths of a second in the close-enveloping fog and snow-laden air. The numbers on the timing clocks changed steadily, clocking off tenths and hundredths of a second as the small figure drew ever closer to the beckoning finish line. Viewers in the United States crossed their fingers against the chance that a slight failure in judgment might send the crouching, graceful figure into an awkward, fallen puppetlike sprawl that would end this odyssey.

But Barbara kept coming, kept hitting the gates just right, kept poles and skis working together effortlessly. Finally she was through the final string of gates and putting all her strength into a last all-out push over the few hundred yards to the goal. Then she was through and making her sweeping turn in front of the picket fence behind which were the fans. All eyes turned to the scoreboard which lit up almost instantaneously with a string of figures that showed the name "Cochran" in first place by a fragile 0.002 second. But it surely was enough for though many others were still to try their hand against the clock, none were close enough in first run time to overtake the petite blonde from Vermont.

Teammates, including the other Cochran children, streamed over to her, shaking her hand, patting her on the back, then lifting her onto their shoulders and marching around in a victory dance. Back in Vermont, her parents were proud and pleased but Mickey, a coach to the last said, "It was almost perfect. But she did run a little wide in the gates."

11

MICKI KING
Diving

One sport in which women have excelled for a good many years is the demanding one of diving. But few have compared with Maxine Joyce "Micki" King, who not only dominated the field in the late '60s and early '70s, but on more than one occasion proved she could compete on equal terms with the male diving stars.

The art of diving might be thought of as a combination of ballet and acrobatics. It requires grace and symmetry. The motions of arms, legs and torso have the flowing artistry of dance. But physical requirements are also crucial. Sustained muscular effort is a must—combined with split-second timing—for the diver to push off the vibrating springboard or the rigid platform at just the right moment and with the correct amount of upward momentum. The diver must propel his or her body high enough so the desired kinds of mid-air gyrations can be performed, but far enough away from the starting point to avoid hitting the now-menacing outline of the board or platform on the way down.

Few individuals of either sex have reflexes needed

for springboard diving, which takes place from a board only some three meters above the water surface. Fewer still have the courage to try even a feet-first drop from the ten-meter-high platform that rears the equivalent of two stories high over the rippling pool waters. To see an accomplished diver climb the long ladder to the high dive position, then effortlessly push off to soar for split seconds in free space before plunging down in a limpid swan dive or spinning ball-like through one, two or more rolls before straightening out for a knife-edge entry is a memorable sight. The onlookers applaud the spectacular feat while feeling an inward sigh of relief at not having to dare such a barrier on their own.

Despite this, there has never been a lack of girls wanting to test themselves against the demands of diving. When Micki King took up the sport, she was heir to a tradition of excellence established by many previous American champions.

Born and raised in Pontiac, Michigan, Micki showed skill at sports in her early years. When she was a few years old she had unusually good co-ordination, and by the time she was going to elementary school she could throw a ball as well as most of the boys in her class. She also showed skill at the winter sports common to the region and her mother thought she might have the makings of a figure skater. Micki dutifully began taking lessons but soon balked at continuing. The painstaking requirements of performing precise "school figures" and the constant repetition of the turns and pirouettes seemed too restrictive. She was bored by it all and just refused to go on.

Diving, on the other hand, thrilled her. Even as a

ten-year-old, she looked forward to the challenge of defying gravity and the breathtaking sweep of downward flight. But it was more than that. She just felt at home in the water. She went swimming whenever she had the chance and joined the swim team when she went to high school. She enjoyed the rough and tumble of water sports and was attracted to water polo, often going as a spectator to watch boys' water polo games.

For most of her early teens, she practiced springboard diving just for the fun of it. It was not until she was fifteen that she actually competed against other girls. She entered a competition at the Toledo YMCA, having practiced dives she had learned from reading books and articles or from watching others do them. Micki felt self-conscious, even awkward until she began to perform. Then everything seemed to fall into place. To her surprise, she placed first even though, as she said later, she knew she had a lot to learn; she didn't even know what her dives were called.

But diving remained more of a hobby than a sport until she went to the University of Michigan in 1962. She tried out for girls' water polo and made first string goalie in short order. By the end of her freshman year she was recognized as one of the best female water polo players in the United States.

Dick Kimball, coach of the water polo team, also headed the swimming team, and Micki began to dive seriously under his watchful eye. He was impressed with her raw talent, although she was far from a world-class performer. He had faith in her potential, though most diving experts would have considered her chances for greatness slim. She was, in effect, just starting to learn the basics of the sports at an age when some of the greatest divers were at the height of their career. She had been diving for nine years, but not on a steady, competitive basis. Most of the great divers devote hours to training from their early years and are taking part in national and international competition by their mid-teens.

For Micki, platform diving was an almost completely new experience at that time. Except for an occasional straight jump from a high board, she had done little of this nature before. As she told William F. Reed of *Sports Illustrated,* "I would like to know what makes people jump. A lot don't at first, you know. They stand there on the edge and finally walk away. Height is the big psychological thing that scares people off. When you hit the water after jumping off the tower, you're going about forty miles an hour. Sometimes you hit with such force that your shoulders and upper arms turn black and blue. I was scared for three years."

Scared or not, Micki rapidly learned the rudiments of both platform and springboard diving and became the mainstay of the Michigan women's team from 1963 to 1966. In her sophomore year Micki became the sensation of Big Ten diving competition. She was close to unbeatable in both springboard and platform diving with a predictable series of flawless, breathtaking dives that won her marks of 8 or 9 points, sometimes even a 9+ from almost all judges of major competitions. (In diving, as in skating and gymnastics, scoring is done on a basis of 10 points for a perfect dive. A judge awarding 7 or 8 indicates it was a good dive while a 9 or better indicates an exceptional performance.) As a junior, Micki did even better, not only bringing many victories for her school, but going on to bask in the national spotlight as the winner of the Amateur Athletic Union indoor platform-diving crown.

Her brilliance as a performer was predictable. What was unpredictable were some of the variations she sometimes came up with, intricate dives that had never been successfully tried in competition before. One such effort that brought exclamations of awe from experts was her 1964 back 1½ somersault with 2½ twists. In this dive, she vaulted from the platform to grasp her legs firmly against her body and whirl in the air a full 360 degrees and then another 180 degrees. Still high above the surface, she then snapped out full length and twisted her body around and around two full times and a half. Despite all of these actions, she still had the time to pull her arms together and enter the water perfectly perpendicular to the surface. It was an addition that insured higher scores by increasing the "degree of difficulty" factor.

In this sport the basic rating for execution of a dive is adjusted to take this into account. If a dive is considered more complex than certain basic dives, it may be assigned a factor of 2 or 3. The point total awarded for a dive is multiplied by the difficulty factor to determine the overall score. If the judge awards an 8, for instance, for the way the dive is performed, with a degree of difficulty of 2, the diver would gain 16 points; with 3, 24 points, and so on.

Growing steadily more proficient, Micki looked eagerly forward to the goal of any great diver, a chance for the gold medal in the Olympics. A vital question, though, was how she would be able to support herself and still devote the many hours of time needed in practice and competition to prepare herself for the next Olympic opportunity. The United States provides no special financial aid for its top amateur athletes; about the only nation involved in Olympic competition that doesn't. Nor could Micki ask her family to sacrifice to keep her free for sports. She also knew an eight to five job wasn't the answer. It would be hard to find one that would offer the flexibility of time off to attend meets all over the country.

Helped by Don Kimball, Micki pondered the matter for many months before completing her college career in mid-1966. Finally she found a way. She enlisted in the Air Force as an officer candidate. The Air Force was interested in the publicity it might gain from having one of its own—an international champion such as Micki—diving against the world's finest divers.

After Micki received her 2nd lieutenant's commission in the fall of 1966, she was assigned to work with the Reserve Officers Training Corps at her alma mater. There she could continue her training under Kimball's watchful eye. Even so, Micki provided the service with a full week's work for a full week's pay. She was allowed to adjust her schedule to take time off when a big meet was coming up, then make up for it at another time.

With Kimball lending encouragement, Micki undertook an even tougher regimen than in the past. She swam many miles a week, religiously exercised to tone and strengthen her muscles and went over every dive in her repertoire again—and again—and again. Between practice and her Air Force work, there was little time left for socializing or entertainment. Each day was a full one with enough physical exertion to match what the average person might undergo in weeks or months. And when it was over, it was generally early to bed with no time for a movie or even a TV show. But for Micki it was worth it. Mexico City and the opportunity of a lifetime beckoned in the summer of 1968.

In countless meets in 1967 and '68 Micki demonstrated her mastery of the diving art. At the relatively advanced age of twenty-three, she easily outpointed lithe young mermaids four, five or six years her junior. By the time the Olympic trials came in mid-1968, Micki was in superb form and unquestionably the outstanding United States performer in three-meter springboard. When lists of possible medal winners at Mexico City were compiled, Micki's name was always prominently displayed.

There were, admittedly, a few moments of nervousness when Micki arrived at mile-high Mexico City, but none of this was evident when the diving program got underway. Crowds jamming the swim hall exclaimed in amazement at Micki's magnificent combination of spins and twists as she completed her preliminary dives to near perfection. As expected, she swept into the finals and started right off with strikingly beautiful required dives that put her well ahead of the field when the optional part of the competition began. With her unmatchable repertoire of high degree of difficulty stylings, it was hard to see how she could lose.

And as the finals moved along, everything remained bright for Micki. Each time she stepped out onto the board, took her position on the tip and gathered her energy for the jump off, the crowd leaned forward in anticipation. She rewarded them with dazzling moves that coaxed a steady string of high marks from the multinational panel of judges. The most accomplished springboard artists in the world gave their all to match her without success. Each series of dives left Micki a fraction of a point farther in front of the field. Finally, with only two dives left, she could take the gold even with efforts that would win only average ratings.

Micki stepped on the board and took a stance facing inward, her hands stretched forward toward the wall. The dive was a reverse 1½, one she had done hundreds of times before. She tensed, sprang up in the air and immediately sensed she'd put too much into it. She was rising too fast and wouldn't have enough time to complete the revolutions unless she slowed down. Instinctively, in a fraction of a second, she moved her arms to compensate. But when she did, her left forearm hit the board. Fighting a sinking feeling, Micki managed to complete the dive. Her execution was far below normal and she knew it would cost her dearly in points, but worse still, the shuddering pain in the arm told her she might not be able to come back for her last dive.

As Micki rose to the top of the pool, shook her head savagely and swam slowly to the ladder, the judges held their rating cards in the air. There were a few sevens, but most were lower—one as low as 4½. The blinking light on the scoreboard told the story. Micki's total had fallen off badly, enough to cost her the lead.

With one dive to go she could make it up and most onlookers fully expected she would. But they might have thought otherwise if they could have seen the lines of pain in Micki's face in the dressing room. She refused to quit or let herself be taken to a hospital for X rays. Steeling herself to the waves of pain that swept through the arm, she returned to the board to attempt a reverse 1½ somersault with 1½ twists. It was far from easy in the best of circumstances. Micki managed a fair effort, but it wasn't good enough against the best divers in the world. She lost still more ground and finished a dismal fourth. She had missed not only the gold, but all medal awards.

Afterward, a medical examination disclosed she had made the last dive with a broken bone in her arm. It had been a courageous act to continue at all. Still, it was small solace for what seemed like the end of a dream Micki had pursued for so many years. Unable to take part in any sports for the next three and a half months with her arm in a cast, Micki went about her Air Force work as best she could. Now that the most valued award of all seemed to have eluded her, she decided it probably was time to retire. She was considered over-age for a diver already and would be even more so by the next Olympics.

This was her frame of mind when she was transferred to Los Angeles Air Force Station where she had the responsibility of handling funds for athletic equipment and other miscellaneous items. As her arm healed, her spirits picked up and she became interested in what was happening in aquatics. She traveled to Long Beach one weekend to watch the indoor national diving competition in early 1969 and wanted so much to take part she could have screamed from frustration. She made up her mind to start practicing again and received strong backing for her efforts from Dick Kimball and the Air Force sports office in Randolph Field, Texas.

The Randolph Field staff also suggested Micki enter the World Military Games scheduled for Pescara, Italy, later in the year. It meant that Micki would be the only woman taking part in an otherwise all-male event. Even though she would have to learn some new kinds of dives usually only performed by the opposite sex, Micki eagerly accepted. Within weeks she was back at the old training grind and after her enforced layoff, it was a pleasure to feel her body responding to the demands of rigorous exercise. The several months of inactivity had not dulled her reflexes to any extent; when the time arrived to go to Europe, Micki felt strong and confident.

As the diving competition progressed, Micki's exciting maneuvers off both springboard and platform won grudging admiration from even the stubbornest traditionalist. She didn't outpoint all her rivals, but scored well enough to win third place and a bronze medal in platform diving and barely missed equaling it in springboard.

When she returned home, she told her coach she believed she was well able to make the next Olympics in 1972. As the months went by, she proved it again and again with almost faultless performances at a series of major meets. In 1970, she won the AAU outdoor diving championship and proceeded to vanquish the field for two more outdoor crowns in '71 and '72. In early 1972, with the Olympic gold as incentive, she also won the AAU indoor crown and then warmed up for the big games by representing the United States in both platform and springboard at the Pan-American Games.

At the qualifying trials for the Olympics in the summer of '72, Micki put on a great show of superlative diving and qualified in both springboard and platform for Munich.

Still, there were some who wondered aloud if Micki could reach the final pinnacle. She was, after all, twenty-seven years old and she would be up against agile and eager young divers eight to ten years her junior. And the pressure might tell, even on someone with her wealth of experience. Not only was the world spotlight on her, with a billion or so seeing the Olympics on TV, there was also the hard-to-erase memory of the calamity at Mexico City.

If any of this troubled Micki, it was hard to tell from her preparations. Her practices went smoothly and she demonstrated in several pre-Olympic meets that she still was the best the United States could boast.

The script unrolled much like Mexico City once the diving competition got underway. With breathtaking jumps—soaring swan dives, sparkling reverse 1½s, 2½s, forward spinning somersault tucks—she swept through the preliminaries and made the finals. In springboard she demonstrated early she was the one to beat as she steadily won the uproarious approval of the crowd and consistently top marks from the judges. With only two dives left, she had the gold in her grasp barring a mishap as shattering as four years ago. But this time—

for Micki at least if not for that blood-spattered Olympics—the cards were in order. She hit her next to last dive perfectly, the reverse 1½ layout that had been so costly before. And her last dive won resounding applause even from her opposing divers. She rose from the board like an unwinding spring, tucked her legs against her body and rotated dizzyingly but precisely, then uncurled into a tight twist followed by a picture-book entry.

After the award ceremony, Micki looked appreciatively at her newly won medal. "This is very heavy, but I love every ounce of it. I've been diving for eighteen years, longer than the girl who came in second has lived. I kind of felt it was a sure thing going into my last dive."

It was a well-deserved gold for Micki, a fitting climax to a diving career that had made her unquestionably the best woman diver in the world and obviously the equal of all but a handful of male champions.

12

MARY DECKER
Track

A visitor to Orange High School in Southern California in early 1974 watched the boys track team going through its warm-ups. As the boys, most of them tall, strong-looking individuals, jogged around the field in their light-colored sweat suits, they were joined by a slight wisp of a girl whose dark-colored shirt had the letters U.S.A. across the chest rather than the word "Orange" of the others.

The onlooker wondered aloud if the tiny female runner was a mascot or one of the first to break the sexual barriers in high school athletics. A student standing nearby looked surprised for a moment, then pointed out it was Mary Decker. She was working out with the team because she was a sophomore at the high school, but she wasn't a member, though the boys and the high school coach, Lanny Carter, would have welcomed her presence. As Carter told a Los Angeles *Times* reporter, "We'd love to have her on our team, but all we can offer her is a trip to Mission Viejo, not New York or Moscow."

For the little brunette speedster, just over five feet

tall and weighing only ninety-five pounds at the time, was already ranked as one of the best runners in the world. Many experts predicted that by the time she was in her twenties she might well become the greatest woman runner of all time. By then some thought she might be so fast that she could overcome the strength advantage of the opposite sex and be a match for them on their own terms. Certainly her times compared favorably with many outstanding boys in high school competition. In the half mile, for instance, Mary's best of 2:02.4 had been bettered by only two boys on the Orange team; one had clocked 1:54.3 and the other 2:00.1. As Carter noted, when she got to be that age, her time figured to be 1:54 or better.

The small bundle of energy that was Mary Decker, who looked too tiny at fifteen to be in high school, had demonstrated startling speed as a child in California, where she was born in 1958. She was outpacing both boys and girls before she was close to her teens and did so well that her mother enrolled her in the local Blue Angels Track Club. She had already represented that amateur club in a number of meets, running well against girls years older than she was, when she entered high school in the fall of 1972. Under the direction of Blue Angels coach Don DeNoon, she rapidly developed into a world-class runner and was the subject of many articles in track and field magazines by the time she was a teenager.

For DeNoon it meant a great deal of recognition throughout the sports field, but it also meant additional emotional strain. As he told a reporter, "Being responsible for the number one female runner in the world—at least in her events—has to cause extra pressure. I've got to be sure she's on top at the right time and I've got to make sure no mistakes are made in training." It was a tightrope, he knew, because other runners and coaches were likely to challenge any errors he made with so young and great a prospect. Even if he did everything exactly right, sooner or later Mary probably would be placed in the tutelage of a coach with wider experience on world-competitive levels.

But Mary herself caused him few problems, except possibly for her bubbling enthusiasm for her sport. She seemed to thrive on the rugged training regimen that might cause other athletes to fuss and grumble. Her grit and determination, for instance, impressed her fellow athletes at Orange High. As one of them pointed out, "When I first heard she was out for track, I thought she might be out here to show us up, but she changed my opinion. She talks to everyone just like she's a part of the team." In the practice sessions at the high school, no one worked up more of a sweat than Mary, and when she got through there, she went with her mother to the Fountain Valley High School track (ten miles south of the Los Angeles County border) for the Blue Angels practices. After some limbering up exercises her usual routine then was to run all sorts of combinations under DeNoon's guidance. Sometimes this involved a series of sprints, some 440s, 220s, even some dashes followed by some middle-distance turns. At other times she might run several longer distances, one or two miles, alternating with other shorter lengths. Much of the time, she simply raced the clock, but every now and then she would be matched in lanes against several other girls to get experience in competition.

The combinations varied, but it all added up to many miles of running, day in, day out. As with anyone aspiring to sports greatness, it meant giving up a lot of things the average boy or girl valued highly. There was little time for hanging around a malt shop in the afternoon or taking part in school activities, though Mary still rode her bicycle to the store on errands for her mother and earned pin money by weekend baby-sitting. It was a grind that some observers, even including her mother, worried might cause her to lose interest in running before she really reached her prime.

But Mary indicated she didn't think it would happen, mainly because running was fun to her. It came naturally, she noted, like walking or breathing, and her style, one of the most flowing, effortless-looking ones experts had ever seen, bore out her evaluation. By the time she was fifteen, coaches all over the world were studying slow motion movies of her races to see if they could learn something to improve the techniques of their own runners.

During the 1972–73 season, when Mary was fourteen, she proved herself adept at distances from the half mile (880 yards) on down. She starred both outdoors on dirt and cinder tracks and indoors on the hardwood boards set up for important races in major sports arenas. Running against other high school girls she won almost every race she entered by wide margins in times that indicated she would be setting world's records before long. As word of her talent got around, her presence at a meet devoted mainly to college level runners could go a long way to insuring a capacity crowd. Before the season was over, her name was often mentioned in the same breath as twenty-year-old Francie Larrieu, America's great woman distance runner. (By the end of 1973, Francie held the world's record for the women's 1,500 meters, 2 miles and 3,000 meters.) Francie herself suggested that Mary might eventually rewrite the record books for most events, including the mile run.

As the 1973–74 indoor season came along, Mary was a national celebrity, her potential and early exploits being trumpeted to the public on network TV sports programs. Despite that, she seemed outwardly to be taking it all in stride, though her reaction to a pushing incident in a U.S.-Russian meet in Moscow demonstrated she had plenty of turbulent emotions beneath her surface calm. Her practice times continued to improve and DeNoon felt confident the season would turn out to be one of her greatest. During the winter months, she followed a schedule of roughly one meet a week. DeNoon tried to hold her to entering only one race each time, but her enjoyment of running and her exuberance over competing weren't easy to cope with. On several occasions, after Mary pressed for the chance to run in a shorter race—the 440, for instance, or one leg of the mile relay—in addition to the half mile, DeNoon gave in and let her enter two events.

Mary's standing in the track world was underlined by the invitations that flooded DeNoon's desk as he prepared plans for the 1973–74 season. The organizers of all the most glamorous amateur indoor track meets, from New York's famous Millrose Games to the

Los Angeles Times Indoor Games, sought to have Mary on their list of entrants. None of the invitations suggested she take part in any high school level races; she was wanted as a featured participant in the open races.

It was heady praise even for someone several years Mary's senior, but she seemed to take it in stride. When she took her prerace bow at the Millrose Games for the 1,000 yards, she got a ringing ovation from the track-wise crowd. When the gun went off, she worked her way to the front by the end of the first lap around the wooden oval and stayed there as some of the best 1,000-yard runners in the Amateur Athletic Union's ranks fought to stay close. When Mary broke the tape, the applause and roar of approval rang like thunder through the smoky Madison Square Garden air. Mary was clocked in an excellent 2:27.4 with Robin Campbell of Sports International Track Club second in 2:29.9. Few women could point to time any better than Mary's, and later in the season, no one could because Mary set a new indoor record of 2:26.7 seconds.

Two weeks later, Mary received similar acclaim from home-area fans as she took her place at the start of the women's 880-yard run in the Times Indoor Games at the Los Angeles Forum, home of the Los Angeles Lakers basketball team and the Los Angeles Kings pro hockey club. She was part of a stellar program that included such people as sub-4-minute-miler Tony Waldrop and the Oregon distance great Steve Prefontaine. But none of them were as eagerly awaited as the little girl from Garden Grove.

When most of the fans looked at their program, they felt a little let down. Though the race organizers

had tried, they had not been able to line up a field
likely to give Mary much competition. It wasn't that
the other girls were poor runners, just that few women
in the track world could match the amazing times being posted by the rapidly improving youngster. Barring
an injury, Mary figured to win easily, which usually
means the pressure to set a new world's record is lack-
ing.

When the gun went off, Mary quickly moved to the
front and steadily widened the gap between her flying
feet and that of the next runner. She ran without any
obvious strain, so fluidly it was hard to believe she was
going exceptionally fast. But as those fans with stopwatches studied the dials and the announcer reported
the lap times, it was obvious she was setting a blistering pace. At the halfway mark, Mary was twenty or
thirty yards in front and was several tenths of a second
ahead of the world's indoor mark. Sensing a dramatic
result, the crowd picked up its vocal tempo, trying with
the loud encouragement to push the speeding girl to a
new pinnacle. Mary continued to flash over the dark
green-colored track divided into narrow lanes by the series of white lines. At the three-quarter mark, she was
still ahead of the record. The crowd raised its volume
still more and she seemed to respond with more effort.
Finally the last lap came up. The starter raised his
gun as Mary came out of the banked turn and down
the home straightaway. The report of the blank shell
indicating the "gun" lap reverberated through the
arena as Mary swept into the last hundred yards. Sure-
footedly she made her way across the final stretch with
no one closer than half a lap to her darting form. The

officials stretched the white tape across the finish line as Mary rounded the last turn and headed for home. Split seconds later she hit the tape, dragging the thin white cord with her as the approval of the crowd reached a crescendo. When the officials completed checking the time, an expectant hush fell over the audience. The deep voice came over the loudspeaker: "In the women's 880-yard run, first place, Mary Decker in 2:06.7—a new world's record."

Flashing a warm smile to reporters afterward, the glare of flashbulbs glinting off the braces on her teeth, Mary played down her achievement. "I didn't go all out. I can see going under two minutes for sure outdoors." It was an interesting projection. Few men could run much under two minutes, and the world record for the 880, at the time, was a little over 1 minute 43 seconds.

The very next week Mary had the chance to show how accurate that forecast might be. She helped draw a capacity crowd for a Sunday evening indoor meet at the San Diego Sports Arena. Both press and TV eagerly sought her out before the meet and the afternoon paper featured a write-up and pictures on the front page. Again efforts to find opponents with 880 times approaching hers proved fruitless, and once more Mary's only competitor would be the clock.

Naturally, as in Los Angeles, Mary hoped to do something unusual for what she considered to be her hometown crowds. Her prime goal, of course, was to come in first. But, as she told a reporter, "If a record seems within my reach, I'm going to try to break it. Otherwise I'll just run to win."

Young as she was, Mary had already developed some superstitions. One of these was to always eat the same meal before a race. That evening, in San Diego, she sat down to her dinner favorite for race nights, a plate of spaghetti without meat sauce. She arrived at the track well before her race was to be called and watched some of the earlier events. After a while, she put on her spiked shoes and went through her warm-up exercises in the infield.

By the time the call came for the 880, she was warmed up and indicated to DeNoon that she was feeling fine. Once more onlookers could detect a sense of anticipation ripple through the audience as Mary's small figure moved onto the track. Athletes limbering up on the sidelines stopped to watch the race and some of the top names in the track world, including Prefontaine and Francie Larrieu took up positions for a good view. Polite applause was given to the other 880 entrants, who included Ms. Shellhouse from Mary's Blue Angels team and an above-average half miler from San Diego State named Poor. But when Mary's name was called and she ran a few steps forward to acknowledge it, the cheers were deafening.

When the gun went off to start the race, Mary took charge almost immediately, forging to the front and building up her lead with each circle of the track. The other girls tried to match her pace, but to no avail. After two laps she was a few yards ahead; and after four, more than ten yards, and from then on it was only a question of how good a time she would set. As she blazed past the line at the halfway point, the coach signaled her time was fast. The announcer's voice boomed out the figures and the crowd erupted in greater volume as they realized she was doing better than the week before. With a faint smile on her face, her brunette hair plaited into short pigtails that bobbed up and down on the back of her head, Mary increased her speed a bit, lapped one runner and drew closer to another. At the six-lap mark, she was still ahead of the record and the crowd clamored for more. Around the oval she sped as the second hands on the timers' watches clicked their way around the dial. The gun lap came up and, showing no signs of weariness, Mary responded to the pistol crack with another burst of speed. A few tens of seconds later she was past the far straight and into the final turn with sensing devices and hand-held instruments monitoring her progress into the final ten yards. Seven yards from the tape, her time was noted for the 800 meter distance as she streaked for the finish line. In a blur of motion she hit the tape and slowed down to take a victory lap before the wildly cheering throng.

Word buzzed through the assemblage that she probably had set a new record. As Mary wiped the sweat away and accepted congratulations from her teammates and friends, everyone kept one ear cocked for the announcement of her time. Finally it came. For the 880 yards, the loudspeaker boomed, 2:02.4, a new world's record. And the time for 800 meters was 2:01.8, also the fastest ever recorded for a woman.

Mary needed only one thing more for a successful season. Her goal, she had said when the indoor meets began, was to win the 880 in the National AAU indoor championships in New York and thus earn a place on the U.S. squad scheduled to meet the Russians in Moscow in the beginning of March.

Competing against some of the best the United States and Canada had to offer, she took a little longer than usual to move in front, but in the second lap she took the lead as the field stayed much closer than she was used to. The nationally televised race turned out to be a cliff-hanger with Canada's Abby Hoffman challenging Mary on the last lap. But Mary fought her off and won by four-tenths of a second. It was short of her 880 record the week before in San Diego, but good enough for the trip to Russia.

In Moscow, Mary proved her world-class caliber by streaking to victory in the 800 meters. Things were not so wonderful in the mile relay, though. Anchoring a strong foursome, Mary seemed in good position to take the lead when the Russian girl seemed to jostle her. Mary lost stride and fell behind, then angrily threw her baton to the ground. For the first time, Mary was subjected to cries of derision from the partisan crowd. The officials disqualified the Russians for the shoving incident, but also the U.S. team for Mary's fit of anger. Tears flowing down her cheeks, looking the young girl she really was, Mary noted she had been poked in the stomach with the baton in a race she felt sure she would have won. It was a low point, but by the time she was back home, she had banished the frustration from mind and was looking forward to the challenge of the outdoor season.

Some experts had suggested that Mary's intense devotion to her sport might shorten her career. Steve Prefontaine, for one, thought she might burn herself out before she reached what should be her best years. But other runners and coaches pointed to her "fantastic attitude." Coach DeNoon said, "She's got goals other people have never dreamed of having. I learned long ago never to underestimate her."

Mary said, "If my determination and drive stays, I'll keep going. If it falters, then people will say I'll be burnt out." But she indicated she expected to excel for years to come. "It takes a lot to burn out the human body."

13

THERESA SHANK
Basketball

Theresa Shank? Ask anyone you meet, man or woman, boy or girl, and the result probably would be a blank stare. Mention the name Kareem Jabbar or Bill Walton and immediately familiar images flash across peoples' minds. They recall dozens of times they've seen those individuals on TV or caught their names in a newspaper headline. Yet were the pendulum of sport correctly balanced, Theresa Shank's name would awaken equivalent reaction. She is, in other words, to women's basketball what the other two are to men's— the acknowledged best center in her sport.

Not that she looks it. With long brown hair framing her face, in street clothes she's more likely to be taken for a high-fashion model. By male standards she hardly seems tall enough to play guard or forward on championship teams, but at 5 feet, 11 inches, she towers over most girls and, like most outstanding basketball players, her tremendous leaping ability allows her to effectively add many inches to her height compared to the average woman basketballer.

Theresa seemed to take to athletics as soon as she

was old enough to know what games were all about. It was partly the fact that her father, who worked in a local A&P warehouse near the family home in Glenolden, Pennsylvania, loved sports, but it was mainly that she was born with excellent co-ordination and could pick up the ins and outs of sports rapidly. She could outrun many of the boys in elementary school, could throw a ball with power and accuracy and wasn't afraid to ask to join some of the games of the neighborhood boys.

As she told Jane Gross of *Sports Illustrated,* she hosted impromptu basketball games at her home before she reached her teens. "There were five boys on the block, so I was the sixth player and I wasn't very tall then. We played behind my house, shooting the ball between the telephone wires and the kitchen window. When I was thirteen, my father put up a court. I went through an awful lot of loafers in those days because I was too embarrassed to wear sneakers."

The boys (one of whom, Karl Grontz, she later married) may have felt qualms about playing with a girl, but if so, this was overcome by their respect for Theresa's ability. She was a tough competitor, could score in a number of ways and quickly developed skill on defense. The many days of back-yard activity was evident when she tried out for the junior high school team which played in the Catholic Youth Organization League. She was a starter from the time the coach watched her practice, but she found the restrictions of organized girls' basketball hard to endure after the give and take of the boys' version. Harking back to the old concept that girls were too delicate to be exposed to the more rugged aspects of athletics, the rules at the time limited the girls game to half court, to only three dribbles and so on. Luckily, all this changed soon after and the present version of girls' basketball is almost identical with that played by boys.

Even under the stifling conditions that existed then, Theresa stood out as an exceptionally skilled player. Her friends and teammates, most of whom attended the local Cardinal O'Hara High School, were happy when she entered that school, though she wasn't a Catholic. Her presence was soon felt by other Catholic League teams. The Cardinal O'Hara team, with Theresa dominating the backboards and scoring with deadly accuracy from outside and inside, proved almost unbeatable when she was in her sophomore year. By the time she graduated in June 1970, the school had won league titles three out of four years. Its overall record during her years of high school play was 82 won and only 9 lost.

As graduation time approached, Theresa gave little thought to continuing her basketball career. However, her coach, Cathy Rush, was offered the coaching post at Immaculata, a girls' school near Philadelphia run by members of the order of Servants of the Immaculate Heart of Mary. At Cathy's urging, Theresa enrolled in the school as did several girls she had played with or competed against in high school.

As Cathy Rush and her star pupil got used to their new surroundings, they had little idea of what lay ahead. Cathy, of course, could feel that girls' basketball was coming into its own. More girls were interested in playing, and more colleges and universities were fielding teams. In the Philadelphia area in particular, the girls' game had started attracting attention several years earlier. By the end of the 1960s, the championship for the local area was held in a major auditorium, the Palestra, and more than 6,000 fans made the rafters ring as the teams fought for supremacy.

However, despite Theresa's awesome talent, neither she nor her coach thought of national championships when the team met for its first drills in the fall of 1970. A small school, Immaculata had never been too successful in its own league, much less against colleges with long-established winning traditions. As for the outside world, including girls' basketball circles, few were even aware Immaculata existed.

But by the time Theresa was a sophomore and the starting center on the team, the situation had begun to change. Under Cathy Rush's direction, things had started to fall into place in her very first year. The girls who'd worked under her before were aware that she emphasized hard work, good conditioning and attention to basics. The girls had to run lengthy wind sprints at each session and spend a lot of time going over the fine points of the game—over and over again.

As Cathy says, "I guess I'll have to say I'm a demanding coach. Our practice lasts for ninety minutes to two hours and I stress defense. We practice defense until it comes out of our ears. Offenses are hot and cold, but our stability is our defense." This rigorous training, in line with that advocated by the best coaches of male teams, went far beyond that of most girls' teams of the early 1970s. A few girls grumbled, but Theresa took to it readily, knowing it would pay off in competition. And it did, as Immaculata compiled a highly respectable 10–2 record in the 1970–71 season. It brought the school a local reputation, though none of the organizers of the Association for Intercollegiate Athletics (AIAW) would have included the team on any prospective list of tournament invitees.

By the fall of 1971 a more challenging schedule had been arranged, and Cathy Rush radiated a quiet confidence that it would be an even more outstanding year than the one before. When the season got underway the evidence seemed in her favor. The team easily won its first game and continued to turn back all opposition as the season went along. The Macs, as they were nicknamed, had several good ball handlers and shooters, but the heart of both offense and defense was Theresa. It was rare that she failed to lead her team in scoring in a game; even rarer when anyone on the court picked off more all-important rebounds than she did. As the 1971–72 season neared its close, Immaculata was unbeaten and its name was starting to become more familiar to followers of women's basketball in other parts of the country. As it happened, the Macs lost their final regular season game, but this still left them with a record of 19–1. They were invited to the AIAW national tournament more as an afterthought than because the experts expected them to do well. In the pretournament rankings, Immaculata was unseeded; that is, they were not rated as one of the top ten teams of the competition.

Once play got going, though, the Macs showed

their season record was no fluke. In their turquoise uniforms (which looked more like those worn by girl cheerleaders—short skirts and short-sleeved blouses) with the white "IC" in one corner, they took charge of each game at both ends of the court. When the opposing team got off a shot at the basket, Theresa usually blocked out the opposing center and sprang high in the air to snatch the ball no matter which direction it was deflected from basket rim or backboard. Hardly had her feet hit the hardwood floor than her arm flashed out to deliver the ball in an arrow-straight path to a teammate streaking downcourt. Theresa swiftly followed behind the play, ready to take the ball for a 15- or 20-foot outside jumper or to rush forward to sweep an offensive rebound or work to tip in a missed attempt. During the same period that Bill Walton and his UCLA group were clinching their first national championship in March 1972, Immaculata was being crowned winner of the AIAW event with the required 4–0 record.

For 1972–73, the Macs were no longer ignored. Teams in the East sharpened their skills to try to dethrone the new leaders, just as the top teams in male collegiate play hoped to break the amazing win streak of UCLA. Theresa, of course, provided Immaculata with an automatic advantage over the rest of the field. But in the fall of 1972, Cathy Rush could beam even more as she observed the first practices of a new high-scoring freshman, 5 feet, 5 inches Marianne Crawford. The combination of Crawford and Shank, combined with several other returning veterans, promised a team even stronger than the almost all-winning 1971–72 team.

Eastern papers, radio and TV were attracted to the girls' form of basketball by the growing interest in such teams as Immaculata and New York's Queens College. When the Macs appeared at the Palestra and other large arenas in their home area the spectator turnout often rivaled that of many male college games. Some fans found they actually enjoyed the girls game better because the updated rules of the early '70s came closer to those used in pro ball. In addition to allowing full use of the court by all players—in contrast to earlier women's rules where only two "rovers" were permitted —the 30-second clock was adopted. That is, an offensive team must take a shot at the basket in 30 seconds or lose the ball, a move that speeded up the game (and that probably would have permitted Walton and UCLA to have avoided defeat by North Carolina State in 1974 where Carolina's stalling tactics had a major impact on the outcome).

Throughout the 1972–73 season, Immaculata demonstrated it was a stronger team than the year before, one that could score in many ways and that maintained its poise before larger, more vociferous crowds. The team went through the season undefeated and made it through the regionals to the AIAW tournament held on the Queens College campus in March '73. This time, the Macs started the event ranked number one, though more than a few experts thought the veteran Queens College team, which featured an excellent 5 feet, 11 inches center of its own, Rachel Wells, or the unbeaten Western Washington State team with twenty-two straight victories, might well upset them.

As it turned out, a relatively unheralded Southern Connecticut team posed the main problem. Theresa and her associates began with a strong win over Indiana State University, 59–48, and then polished off Western Washington with surprising ease, 66–53. Southern Connecticut, which had taken part in five straight tournaments, began with a close win over Kansas State, 56–52, and an easier outing against Mercer University of Georgia, 58–45.

When Southern Connecticut and the Macs squared off in the semifinals, few gave the Connecticut girls much of a chance. From the first center jump, though, it became evident that the Macs were in for a struggle. Seizing an early lead, the other team dominated the play from the start and steadily increased it as the game progressed. The Macs trailed by several baskets at the end of the half, though Theresa was doing her usual fine job on the boards with close to a dozen rebounds to her credit. Immaculata fans screamed lustily for their team to turn things around as the teams came back on the court for the third eight-minute quarter. For a little while it looked as if the Macs were coming to life as Marianne Crawford and Theresa scored with picture-perfect plays, but Southern Connecticut doggedly held on, matching the Macs basket for basket, then adding a point or two here and there. At the end of the third quarter, Southern Connecticut was in front by 37–29, a tough gap to close in only eight minutes' time. Instead of getting better, though, things got worse. The Connecticut team was having a hot shooting night. Everything they threw up seemed to nestle down within the basket webbing.

With three minutes to go the score was 43–31. To all appearances, time had run out for the Philadelphia crew. However, Theresa and the others kept their cool, regrouped and suddenly caught fire. Theresa seemed to find extra spring in her legs and swept the boards clean again and again. Just past the three minute mark, the Macs scored to make it 43–33. Seconds later they reclaimed the ball and cut the gap to eight points. Now Southern Connecticut began to press a little and began to miss their shots. Each time, the slim form of Theresa Shank was there, perfectly positioned to wrap her long arms around the basketball.

As the last minutes ticked off, the Macs steadily closed in on their tormentors. Marianne Crawford kept firing with deadly accuracy and Theresa hit several jump shots with a fluid motion reminiscent of the style of the All-Pro guard, Jerry West of the Los Angeles Lakers. Just before the one-minute mark, Immaculata tied the game, then choked off the Connecticut scoring attempt to swiftly move to the other end of the court and score the lead goal.

The game seemed theirs now, but the Connecticut girls marshaled their forces to work the ball back into the Macs territory where they hit for a two pointer with twenty-six seconds left. The score was 45-all. The Macs decided to work for the last shot, knowing the worst that would result would be an overtime period. As the tension rose to fever pitch among the frenzied onlookers, the Macs brought the ball upcourt, passing it around as they closely watched the seconds clicking off. The Connecticut girls guarded as closely as they could without taking the chance of committing a foul. The ball went back and forth between the Macs' forwards and guards as Theresa kept the low post position near the basket. Now the clock showed ten seconds, nine, eight, seven, the ball was dribbled a little by one of the players, then Marianne broke loose to one side as the time went within five seconds. The ball came to her, she set, let fly and the sphere arced gracefully up, then down toward the goal. The roar was deafening as Mac fans prayed it would go and rival fans screamed for a miss. The ball was slightly off target. It hit the rim, bounced up, then suddenly there was Theresa's form high up in the air, fingers outstretched. As her fingertips met the leather surface and pushed it toward the basket the buzzer sounded. The ball moved a short distance and came down in the crisscrossed cords for two points and the nineteenth season win. For Theresa, the statistics showed the story —25 rebounds in the game.

The Queens gymnasium was packed for the final game between the home school and the Macs. Reporters from all New York's major papers were there and even more TV/radio crews. Outside, thousands of people clamored for tickets, but the game was sold out. However, it turned out to be an anti-climax. On the first jump ball, Theresa outreached Rachel Wells to slap the ball to a teammate and soon after the Macs scored the first two points. The Queens Knightees couldn't find their outside shooting touch and the stalwart defense of Theresa and her cohorts choked off Rachel Wells and the Knightees inside game. At half it was 27–18, Immaculata, and early in the fourth quarter the Macs led by 22. Cathy Rush pulled her starters soon after and the final score was a misleading 59–52. When Theresa headed for the bench the last time, friend and foe rose to give her a standing ovation. There was no doubt that she merited the Most Valuable Player Award. Against Queens she scored 22 points and gained 10 rebounds. For the tournament as a whole, she led all others in rebounding with a total for four games of 72 and tournament high scorer with a total of 104 points. With the Queens win, Theresa and the Macs had a win streak of 24, including the two straight national championships. Sports writers called them the "UCLA of the East."

Theresa could not be ignored as a candidate for the U.S. women's team being assembled for the World University Games scheduled for Moscow in August '73. Many people who had heard of her feats knew little else about her before she showed up in Iowa in early summer for tryouts. Thinking in terms of Bill Walton, some were surprised she was 5 feet, 11 inches instead of well over 6 feet. However, once she started playing, doubts were swept aside and she was chosen.

In Moscow, things went reasonably well, although the team started by losing a landslide game to the Russian girls who had the advantage of state support that had permitted them to play together year-round for many years. Still, after that loss, the U.S. team came back to win four straight between August 17–21, including decisions over France, 54–43, Romania

54–47 and Bulgaria, 54–47. This earned them the right to replay the Russians in the finals. Once more, the great edge in experience showed and the United States had to settle for second-place medals. However, Theresa played to good effect and most observers felt if the U.S. team could remain together for a time, the result could be reversed.

The 1973–74 Macs remained a power with Theresa closing out her career with another excellent season. For the third straight year the Macs were regional champs and won the right to defend their title at the AIAW finals held in March '74 on the campus of Kansas State University. The team won its first two games with relative ease, then had a tough challenge from William Penn of Iowa in the semifinals. It was a rugged, see-saw battle, but Immaculata refused to panic and finally pulled it out by a basket, 57–55. Marianne Crawford scored 22 points and Theresa Shank, top rebounder as usual, hit for 18. Before a packed house the next night, the Macs turned back Mississippi College for a third straight national championship, one that eluded the mighty Walton Gang of UCLA that same week. For the tournament, Theresa averaged 18.2 rebounds a game.

With that kind of college career, had Theresa been a man, she would have had to worry about such things as whether to take 1-, 2- or 3-million-dollar offers for her future services.

About the Author

IRWIN STAMBLER is a well-known author and editor in the area of pop music. He has written two major encyclopedic reference works on segments of the pop music field. In past years he was a song writer as well as commentator and writer on pop music for radio. In recent years science and technology have claimed as much of his attention as music. He currently is on the editorial staff of Industrial Research Publications and is also the author of over a dozen books on space and scientific subjects. He makes his home in California with his wife and four children.

920
STA

Stambler, Irwin

Women in sports